Seven Powerful Strategies

for

Overcoming Life Challenges

Tested and Proven Life-Changing Keys

ISBN-13: 978-1-913266-02-8

Other Books by the Author:

A Father's Tender and Compassionate Love – A Love So Tender and Compassionate

Hardcover ISBN 10: 1479772887/ ISBN 13: 9781479772889

Softcover ISBN 10: 1479772879 ISBN/ 13: 9781479772872

Principles Of Resolution – A Practical Step-by-Step Guide to Enable You Identify, Set & Accomplish Your Goals

ISBN 10: 1543063780

ISBN13: 9781543063783

Dedication

This book is dedicated with love to all those who are hurting in the world—who seem to have lost every hope and confidence in life. This is to assure you of a new hope and life... Don't give up just yet! You sure deserve the very best of life!

Foreword

The thing that struck me on reading the contents of this book was that my initial thought that it was a 'Self-Help' book was highly misplaced. The more accurate description would be 'Self-Evaluation' and in a world where we all find ourselves juggling increasingly demanding responsibilities with very little time for recreational activities or indeed reflection, Dr Sylvia Forchap-Likambi is the decisive voice that compels us to take a long, hard look and really see ourselves through honest eyes.

Dr Sylvia, epitomises the adage "Good things come in small packages," and in the period that I have known and worked with her as matron at the GLOBAL VISIONARY WOMEN NETWORK, I can confidently attest to the fact that she lives the seven principles of REFLECTION, PERCEPTION, FOCUS, ACTION, GRATITUDE, ASKING and WISDOM laid out in this book. A tenacious, fearless, passionate, motivated woman with an attitude that often has me wondering how on earth she does it.

Often, in times of adversity, fear, shame, and feelings of hopelessness overshadow the clear thinking necessary to take strategic, effective action. The understanding is often missed that even tiny steps taken at the right time lead to an overall resolution of what sometimes may appear insurmountable personal challenges. This book emphatically reminds us that little drops of water do indeed make a mighty ocean or, if you will, a journey of a thousand miles does begin with a single step.

I recall beginning my tenure as a queen with a zeal that was highly disproportionate to available human, social and financial resources, essentially wanting to save the world while dealing with the unfortunate perception that I must naturally have access to unlimited cash flow and therefore needed no assistance in that arena—a situation that could not have been further from the reality.

It was about three years into my role that I began to experience the frustrations that arose out of an inability to keep up the momentum purely because I was overextended in time, money and energy, needing to keep going for fear of letting a lot of people down. I was definitely on my way to a complete burnout.

Lured by the glamour of the position coupled with a deep need to help people, I had made the fundamental error of giving too much too soon with no backup strategy whatsoever. It took the realisation that I needed to take time out to reflect, evaluate, focus, and ask for help for me to properly appreciate and target my leadership skills. I relinquished the need to say yes to everything and became selective. To do that with any level of success, I had to learn to tune out much of the negativity that inevitably arose out of not being so readily at everyone's disposal.

The result of this change in my personal strategy was that I also discovered the art of true gratitude. Rather than suffer anxiety due to the limited resources available to me, I began to appreciate the fact that at any particular moment I had the ability, by choice, to help in whatever capacity I had been called upon to do so through hard work.

Purchasing this book is an investment in your well-being, success and personal significance. The benefits of applying the strategies taught are life-lasting. I challenge you to go out and grab your copy. I look forward to hearing your testimony.

Queen Naa Tsotsoo Soyoo I

Traditional Ruler from the Ga State of Ghana

Entrepreneur, Philanthropist, Community Leader and Advocate

Table of Contents

Preface

We live in such an era of technology, where we are constantly bombarded with all sorts of information and knowledge—consciously or unconsciously. To a large extent, most of this information is erroneous and does nothing other than instill pain, distress, and/or fear in us! We are constantly exposed to periods of violence, uncertainty, and hopelessness, which sap out almost all the energy from within us, making us very vulnerable, distressed, and fearful—almost all the time! There is virtually no good news out there, despite the many amazing people we have today in our societies doing amazing jobs out there! Our world is losing every sense of purpose and true meaning—and many people seem to just go with the flow and are tossed forward and backwards in whichever direction the wind blows them to. They seem to have lost total control of their lives and being and just let the everyday situations of life or their circumstances shape and determine which way their lives will go, when and how. What a waste of valuable time and life on Earth.

As you prepare to read this book, I would like you to take some time out right now and examine your life today— look at your current life circumstances. Whatever they may be, or may not be, I want you to know that you are blessed and privileged to still be alive today. Life itself is an enormous and precious gift and blessing. And because you are still alive today, there is still hope for you. You are a victor and not a victim of your life circumstances—especially the negative ones. Therefore, do not dwell in self-pity but in self-love and gratitude, looking ahead of you with a brand-new hope and expectation of a wonderful and fulfilling life.

I am very conscious of the fact that you may be going through some really challenging times right now while reading this book—we all have been there at least once if not numerous times in our lives. Therefore, this book is to encourage you, to let you know that you are not alone and what you are going through at the moment is not uncommon or peculiar to you alone—so take heart, rise up, dust yourself off, and walk boldly and confidently today (with your head held high again) towards the path of a fulfilled and happy life.

Happiness is a conscious choice and decision, and you must do everything possible to make the conscious effort to live a happy life – regardless of what life throws at you or brings your way – now and in the future.

I have been contemplating for a while now before finally deciding to write this very vital manual/guide. I pondered and questioned: what could I possibly bring to our generation, and children (who are our future and leaders of tomorrow), that could be of great relevance and contemporary at the same time? I thought and thought and thought... I also enquired of some of the amazing women and men I have been privileged to serve and work with over the years. My intention was to find out from them what piece of information/knowledge could be most relevant and applicable in their lives right now—especially in such challenging and uncertain times with little or no direction or clarity. After speaking with over 100 women and almost 25 men (most of which was done during the month of March, when the world celebrated women and mothers on International Women's Day and Mother's Day, respectively), it was very evident and clear that there was a cry for a timeless guide and message of encouragement to enable women and mothers, and also men (especially parents), to be able to encounter and overcome the everyday life challenges they face with more grace and serenity.

It is very evident that as women, mothers, and parents, our challenges are countless and continuous—they are especially evident when one's package includes being a wife, mother, carer, and/or daughter in-law... That's pretty challenging by itself! Yet, whenever I think of all such challenges, there is this famous quote from Nelson Mandela that constantly comes to my mind:

"After climbing a great hill, one only finds that there are many more hills to climb."

After arriving at the top of the great hill you have just finished climbing and then realising that there are many other hills you still have to climb...What do you do? Do you start complaining? "Life is so unfair... Why me? I am tired and fed up. I can't do this any longer... I give up, give in, and quit!" Oh no! Winners never give up or quit, and quitters never win! Such an attitude will take you to nowhere; rather, it will leave you even more frustrated and resentful! You need to be aware and be able to acknowledge that, after overcoming one giant life challenge, one only gets to find out that there are many more giant challenges to overcome! It is almost never ceasing, with every new level coming with its own brand-new challenges—very well packaged and delivered.

Sometimes, it seems as though every new success comes wrapped up in a gift bag with a token or excess of accompanying challenges! Therefore, you must keep going and giving your all... You must keep pressing on and keep the faith alive—knowing you are always a victor and never a victim of your circumstances/challenges. You should know that you are, or can be, in control—and not let your circumstances or current challenges take control and shape your life and future accordingly.

Having said this, I appreciate you might be asking me, and rightly too, "But how is this possible, Sylvia? Just how? Tell me! You have absolutely no clue what I have been through and what I am still going through at the moment! How dare you berate my situation?"

I tell you one thing... As I sit here writing and addressing you through this book, my very own life and essence of being is the greatest testament to my authority and leadership in this area! I say not a thing to you in this book that I have not applied or do not apply in my own life—with proven results. Furthermore, these same principles and strategies I have shared with hundreds of women and some men going through some of the worst challenges and nightmares you could ever imagine—with proven results and testimonials from many of them.

One very common and frequent question a lot of women and men I have worked with ask me is this: "What is the secret behind your ever-smiling face, confidence, and mental strength/resilience?"

The answer, which I often summarise in a few simple, yet profound words, is this: "In knowing who I am, where I have come from, where I am going to, and being in control of my mind."

Now, in this book I am going to be sharing with you seven profoundly powerful well-tested and proven strategies, which you can adopt from now on and implement whenever you are going through any challenge in life. I have shared these strategies with numerous women and men, and applied them over and over again in my own life—with exceptional and groundbreaking results!

I guarantee, if you apply all or some of these powerful strategies (depending on the gravity of your situation/challenge) in the very order I am going to give them to you, life will be much more fun and glorious to live— amidst the countless and continuous challenges you encounter daily. You will eventually come to an understanding that every single challenge in life is another opportunity to grow, better yourself, and thrive! These strategies are not static, and the amount of time you dedicate and spend on each one of them is variable and will depend on the gravity and severity of your challenge or situation.

Now, what are these fundamental core strategies you need to know and implement each time you encounter or are going through some very challenging situations and moments in life? Let's ride on as we unravel and explore them in the subsequent chapters of this book. Get yourself a drink, sit back, put your feet up, relax, and enjoy the journey...

Acknowledgements

To my darling and beloved husband, Mike—for the wonderful and challenging times spent together. I am especially grateful for every challenging moment encountered with you, as they have been very valuable and pivotal in shaping and transforming me into the amazingly confident and resilient woman that I am today! I am profoundly grateful for having you in my life...With you, I have grown, learned, and become a much better person, and I continue to learn and grow daily. Thank you!

To my amazing and wonderful babies, love, and angels—Latoya, Caleb, and Destiny; with all the challenges and exceptional joy and fulfilment that come with motherhood, I could never have asked for any better! You awesome three are simply the very best any mum could ever ask for and have sure contributed immensely in making me such a resilient and mentally strong woman and friend. With you, I have come to learn that in motherhood, resilience, patience, optimism, and mental stability are not options to choose and pick from, but rather they are obligatory—a must-have! I love you all immensely!

To Her Majesty, Queen Naa Tsotsoo Soyoo I of The Ga State Of Ghana—for your devotion and commitment to Global Visionary Women Network, the people and community, and most especially for honouring and accepting my request to write the foreword of this book, despite your very hectic and busy schedule. I am profoundly grateful!

To my beautiful family, beloved friends, pastor, loved ones, and all the amazing men and women I have been privileged to work with and serve—I profoundly appreciate and celebrate you… Most especially, I am grateful for having you play a very significant role in my life.

Most importantly, to my most gracious and loving Heavenly Father and God, for the indescribable gift of mental strength and tenacity! Thank you for your faithfulness, for always keeping me steadfast, sane, and serene amidst all odds.

"Be still ... taking some time to look within and reflect... There is greatness and power within you to overcome every challenge you are facing right now."

Dr Sylvia Forchap-Likambi

"Reflect upon your present blessings—of which every man has many—not on your past misfortunes, of which all men have some."

Charles Dickens

CHAPTER ONE

The Power of Reflection

"A man must find time for himself. Time is what we spend our lives with. If we are not careful we find others spending it for us. . . . It is necessary now and then for a man to go away by himself and experience loneliness; to sit on a rock in the forest and to ask of himself, 'Who am I, and where have I been, and where am I going?' . . . If one is not careful, one allows diversions to take up one's time—the stuff of life."
Carl Sandburg

Too often, when we encounter life challenges or crises, without any prior knowledge, experience, or expectation, it is

23

but normal to get carried away by the challenging circumstances—without necessarily taking the time out to reflect. More often than not, we tend to react to challenging situations in life rather than respond from a place of rest and expectancy. We are hardly proactive in dealing with life challenges or crises, as they often take us by surprise—without any prior experience or plan in confronting and overcoming any such crises.

When you set out knowing that in this world you will always have challenges, regardless of how excellent or successful you are, then you are in a better position to be prepared to welcome and embrace life challenges—with a very optimistic attitude and approach. In order words, when you expect something to happen, you are better equipped mentally and emotionally to handle and overcome it. Of note, it is written in John 16:33 that "in this world you will have tribulations, so be of good cheer for I have overcome the world."

Reflecting in the midst of challenges or storms is an excellent kick-off strategy for victory—as this gives you, first and foremost, the amazing opportunity to seek the much needed energy and mental strength to equip and prepare you for victory. It gives you the ultimate opportunity to be in control once again—amidst all odds. This is because reflection takes your focus and energy off the crisis or challenge and ensures that your focus is on YOU! It gives you the perfect opportunity to be the author and finisher of your own story, the opportunity to make and be the change you expect to see during and after the situation. It gives you an opportunity to tap from within you, to search deep down within your soul for intuitive guidance and directions. It also gives you the opportunity to be still and shut off all the negative voices and distractions from without. It takes your eyes off the challenge or problem and places them on you and the desired solution/outcome. It gives you the opportunity to think, rethink, strategise, re-strategise, relax, refresh, pray, listen to your inner being/spirit, meditate, be creative, and come out with one or more possible options and a way forward.

"It is when you lose sight of yourself that you lose your way. To keep your truth in sight you must keep yourself in sight and the world to you

should be a mirror to reflect to you your image;
the world should be a mirror that you reflect
upon." C. JoyBell C.

Furthermore, in being still, silent, stepping back, and reflecting, you give yourself the amazing and priceless opportunity to tap into your inner source – your inner spirit – and be in total control. In order words, it ensures that you are not letting your challenges and circumstances take control of you but looking for the power and inner strength to control them from within ... based on who you truly and fundamentally are—your beliefs, core convictions, values, thoughts, actions and habits.

"Without deep reflection one knows from daily life that one exists for other people." Albert Einstein

During this brief or prolonged period of silence/reflection (depending on the gravity and nature of the challenge) a very valuable and practical prayer, which I highly recommend and encourage you to say, is the Serenity Prayer. It comes in very handy and goes like this: "Lord, grant me the serenity to accept the things I cannot change, the courage to the change the things I can, and the wisdom to know the difference." Each challenge in life is an opportunity for you to grow and become wiser—knowing which battles to pick and fight and which to disregard and/or let go for your own sanity. You simply cannot fight every single battle in life; you simply are not equipped and wired to do this. You need to concentrate on what is important and matters to you and redirect your focus on this—for the sake of your health, well-being, and happiness.

This implies wisdom is crucial and indispensable—which is the ability to know and apply the right thing at the right moment. In essence, it is your ability to identify and tell the difference—the difference between which battles you are meant to courageously affront and overcome and which ones to let go of and walk away from with dignity and serenity.

Consequently, whenever you are faced with a challenge, do not immediately react or respond; don't run out there looking for solutions in others. It's an opportunity for you to be still and search inwardly... The duration of this step of reflection or silence will depend on the gravity of the situation at hand or the subsequent consequences that will result from the situation. The more serious the situation and the more weight the consequences will have in your life and future the more time you should allow or think of allowing for reflection and meditation. Whereas, in a very straightforward situation, or in the case of a similar challenge you might have encountered in the past, the less time may be needed to effectively implement this initial strategy.

If you step back and take some time to reflect on this key strategy, you will realise that each time you are confronted with a challenge or problem, you almost always inevitably apply this strategy—most often unconsciously and/or very briefly. What I want you to start doing henceforth, after reading this book, is deliberately incorporate this habit. Irrespective of how long you choose to do so, what is more crucial and fundamental is that you become conscious while you do this as it automatically gives you the power to unleash the resources needed to be in control and at peace.

> *"When you connect to the silence within you that is when you can make sense of the disturbance going on around you." Stephen Richards*

On the contrary, a lot of people end their problem-solving strategy here. They retire to meditating and reflecting, and more often than not, they do so focusing their energy and strength not within themselves and the power within them needed to drive solutions, but rather on the problem and the consequences to follow, if not resolved. This merely becomes worrying, and creates anxiety—which, if prolonged, may lead to depression and become very unhealthy and unproductive. Therefore, it is vital that you do not misinterpret the difference between meditating on a possible strategy and way forward to bring about a solution and meditating on the problem without any strategy or plans whatsoever towards resolution.

Furthermore, the essence of reflection is to give you an opportunity to step back and step aside from the problem. This positions you in a better platform to better view the problem/challenge from every angle and in a very objective manner. It separates you – the subject – from the object and enables you to be able to deal with whatever situation you have at hand objectively. The latter provides you with wider opportunities and options for resolution.

Dr. Sylvia Forchap-Likambi

"We cannot see our reflection in running water. It is only in still water that we can see." Zen Quote.

"We currently live in a fast-paced world where we are constantly on the move... In most instances, the direction of movement seems to have little or no relevance to many—it may be forward, backwards, or even on the same spot... just spinning around, yet this is of little importance. However, it is very vital and fundamental that we take some time to step aside—get off the turbulence, be still, watch, and reflect... In this way we are able to better understand and make sense of what is going on within and around us—before embarking on a direction of movement..." Dr Sylvia Forchap-Likambi

I want you to imagine walking towards a pile of stones right in front of you, which eventually obstructs your view and your path. You will notice that if you stay right there, directly in front of the pile of stones, your view will be obscured, and all you see is the pile of stones with no outlet. However, imagine yourself stepping back a few steps away from the pile of stones, what do you see or notice? You would realise that you are now able to see to the right, left, and most probably the top of the pile of stones. Interestingly, the farther away you are from the pile of stones the more clarity you have, and the better your chances of having a good view of the sides and especially the top. Consequently, you are now able to see those other options available to you, and that will enable you go beyond the obstacle/pile of stones. Eventually, what you initially considered and thought was a stumbling block has now presented itself to you as a stepping stone to take you to a higher platform and altitude, for better positioning to victory.

In addition, have you noticed that the closer you are to the obstacle the larger it seems to appear? While the farther away you are from it the smaller and more diminished it becomes. In other words, the farther away you are or your focus is from the problem or challenge at hand the more diminished and smaller the challenge appears to be! Hence, you must learn to distance yourself from the challenge/problem at hand so it may become diminished and easier to confront and overcome.

In the same manner, walking directly into a closed door that was meant to lead you to your destination or victory can sometimes be very frustrating. Nonetheless, there is always a better side to this, but then you need to be able to see this. If you arrive at the closed door being so frustrated, such that you choose to focus all your strength and energy on the door, banging and kicking it really hard, you fail to see the bigger picture. Such an attitude leads to nowhere but more frustration and pain, or even denial. However, when you choose to step back farther away from the door, there is the possibility that you may see another door or doors and even windows, with someone in the building or surrounding area you could talk to. It might just be that the door was temporary shut with another access point being made available—but without stepping aside and away from the door, you will never be able to see the several opportunities and options presented to you by the shut door.

In the course of stepping back and stepping aside, there needs to be a mind shift—from a mind that is problem-focused to that which is solution-focused. You cannot remain in the same position you were in or with the same mindset you had prior to encountering a problem and expect to resolve the problem in that same position or with that same mindset... Oh no! This is absolutely not possible! There needs to be a mind shift, from problem to solution. How do you do this?

It is very simple—by simply turning over the coin. This eventually leads you to the next powerful strategy required to successfully overcome life storms/challenges, which is changing your perception about the challenges and obstacles you are faced with. It is fundamental that you change your perception about that problem or particular situation you are faced with and look at it from different perspectives—if you want to encounter and overcome it with grace and immense inner strength and serenity.

REFLECTION AND ACTION POINTS

The beginning of every transformation starts with awareness. When you become aware of the fact that there is a genuine need for change – a need for resolution, a need for a mindset shift from problem to solution, from frustration and unrest, to satisfaction and serenity/peace – then you are ready to embark on a transformational journey to bring about the change and outcomes/solutions you desire.

Nevertheless, the starting point should be true in-depth knowledge of yourself as a unique individual and how you relate and respond to your surrounding environment and life challenges. The simple truth is the more you know and understand yourself the better you are able to accept or change who you are, and thus the circumstances around you. Being ignorant or unaware of who you truly are leaves you trapped in your own inner struggles and opens the doors to outside forces/challenging circumstances to mould and shape you accordingly.

Self-awareness requires honesty and courage—in order to genuinely connect with your beliefs, values, perceptions, and emotions and to face the truth about yourself and the situation at hand. Unfortunately, many people are not prepared to face the truth about themselves and so prefer to live in denial or constantly looking for the solutions to their problems in the problems or in others. Or, worse still, they look for what and who to blame whenever they face challenges.

Nonetheless, the first step towards this journey is not becoming aware of the problem or others around you but, rather, becoming aware of YOU and how the current challenge/situation is affecting you. You need to have an introspective view of yourself, your emotions, thoughts, words, actions, etc. to be able to identify how you can better control yourself and effectively manage the challenge at hand and eventually express yourself accordingly.

The aim of this section is to enable you to reflect and identify/establish who you truly are or the fundamentals of who you are and represent. In this way, you may be able to tap within you and explore/exploit the incredible and endless potentials and power that lie within. This will be done by asking and sincerely responding to some very crucial questions about YOU. Below are some of the questions you must ask yourself now; do not wait until you encounter a challenge before you do this. Do it now so that when those challenges come in the future, you already have an in-depth knowledge of who you truly are and therefore remain grounded and rooted in your identity and purpose. It is also beneficial to remind yourself of the answers to these questions whenever you are faced with challenges/adversities.

1. What is/are my core conviction/s and belief/s? Something I strongly believe in and will not compromise.

....

....

....

....

....

....

....

....

....

....

2. What am I ready to do to fall out with man in order to please God or be at peace with myself?

....
....
....
....
....
....
....
....
....
....
....
....

3. What are my greatest strengths?

....
....
....
....
....
....
....

....

....

....

....

4.   What are my weaknesses?

....

....

....

....

....

....

....

....

....

....

....

....

5.   How do close friends, family and loved ones describe me?

....

....

....
....
....
....
....
....
....
....

6.   Do I agree with their descriptions?

....
....
....
....
....
....
....
....
....
....

Why or why not?

....
....

....
....
....
....
....
....
....
....

7. In what situations and/or environments am I most at ease?

....
....
....
....
....
....
....
....
....
....

What specific element/s in these situations/environments makes me feel at ease?

....

....

....

....

....

....

....

....

....

....

8.   What is/are my greatest passion/s in life?

....

....

....

....

....

....

....

....

....

....

Why?

....

....

....

....

....

....

....

....

....

....

9.   What types of activities did I enjoy doing when I was a child?

....

....

....

....

....

....

....

....

....

....

10. What about now? Are these activities different from those I enjoyed as a child?

....

....

....

....

....

....

....

....

....

Why?

....

....

....

....

....

....

....
....
....
....

11. What motivates and drives me most in life?

....
....
....
....
....
....
....
....
....
....

Why?

....
....
....
....
....
....

....
....
....
....

12. What are my dreams for the future (the next 10–15 years)?

....
....
....
....
....
....
....
....
....
....

What steps am I taking to achieve my dreams?

....
....
....
....
....

....

....

....

....

....

13. What do I fear most in life?

....

....

....

....

....

....

....

....

....

....

Why?

....

....

....

....

....

....
....
....
....
....

14. What types of things and situations stress me in life?

....
....
....
....
....
....
....
....
....
....

15. What is my typical response to stress?

....
....
....
....
....

....

....

....

....

....

16. What qualities do I like to see in others and especially
dear and loved ones?

....

....

....

....

....

....

....

....

....

17. Do I have many friends and loved ones with the qualities
and attributes I just described?

....

....

....

....
....
....
....
....
....
....

18. Why or why not?

....
....
....
....
....
....
....
....
....
....
....
....
....

19. When I strongly disagree with someone's point of view, opinion, or ideas, what do I do? How do I express this disagreement/myself? Am I aggressive, assertive or passive?

....
....
....
....
....
....
....
....
....
....

20. Am I willing to liberate myself from the burden and bondage of my past, my life challenge/s and others in similar positions? Remember this, where there is a will there is always a way!

....
....
....
....

....

....

....

....

....

....

21. Am I willing/ready to turn my mess into a message of hope and healing?

....

....

....

....

....

....

....

....

....

....

....

....

22. Am I willing/ready to change, learn, grow, and transform my adversities into my testimonies and life lessons/stories to serve others?

....

....

....

....

....

....

....

....

....

....

23. Whenever I encounter challenging life situations, what is the overall impact on me and my health and well-being?

....

....

....

....

....

....

....

....

....

....

24. After a significant life challenge, who do I become?

....

....

....

....

....

....

....

....

....

....

Do I become:

- Stronger or Weaker?

- Happier or Sad and Depressed? Encouraged or Discouraged?

- Motivated or Demotivated and Uninspired?

25. What are the three most significant life challenges I have encountered and overcome?

1. ....
....
....

2. ....
....
....

3. ....
....
....

26. How did I overcome each one of them?

....
....
....
....
....
....
....
....
....
....
....
....
....

27. What significant lessons did I learn from them and how are they relevant or applicable in my life?

....
....
....
....
....
....
....
....
....
....

28. How will I confront similar challenges in the future?

....
....
....
....
....
....
....
....

Dr. Sylvia Forchap-Likambi

....

....

Why?

....

....

....

....

....

....

....

....

....

....

"Perception is strong and sight weak. In strategy it is important to see distant things as if they were close and to take a distanced view of close things."

Miyamoto Musashi

"The task is...not so much to see what no one has yet seen; but to think what nobody has yet thought, about that which everybody sees."

Erwin Schrödinger

CHAPTER TWO

The Power of Perception

"Miracles happen every day, change your perception of what a miracle is and you'll see them all around you." Jon Bon Jovi

I heard of this story about a young woman and mum who had just gone through a very difficult divorce, lost her family/her only child, and, as if that wasn't enough, also lost her job/was made redundant. Everything seemed to be falling apart in her life, which greatly affected her overall health and well-being—causing her to become depressed and suicidal. She was very resentful and bitter about life and had completely lost every hope in herself and in life.

She had finally decided to take away her life—when, suddenly, she thought of her beloved grandmother (Granny).

59

Her granny is very optimistic, loves life, and often tells her amazing stories of how beautiful life is … and always encourages her to be at her very best and enjoy the goodness of life. Immediately, she felt the urge within to pay her granny one last visit, and use the opportunity to tell her how disappointed and hopeless she was. She wanted to express her profound dismay about the life her granny speaks so well of—she thought she owed this final respect and tribute to her.

"There are things known and there are things unknown, and in between are the doors of perception." Aldous Huxley

On arriving at her granny's house, her granny instantly noticed the sadness and hopelessness on her granddaughter's face and asked her to sit down and tell her what the problem was. As she sat there, talking to her granny about all her frustrations, losses, and disappointments, she was moved to tears. Her granny then comforted her and told her that she would like to take the opportunity to illustrate to her a very profound life lesson. She requested that she paid attention and watched her. She stood and took three pots, all of which were the same size, weight, shape and material. She filled up each one of the pots with the same quantity of tap water (1000 ml each) and heated them all up on the cooker with the same amount of heat for up to 10 minutes—until the water in all three pots was boiling.

At this point, she got a carrot, an egg, and some coffee and put them in the three different pots—one in each. In the first pot, she added the carrot to the boiling water; in the second, she added the egg; and in the third and last pot, she added the coffee and let them cook for an additional 10 minutes. At the end of the 10 minutes, she then took out the carrot, egg, and coffee, and served them on two different plates and in a cup respectively.

After serving them, she placed them on the table in front of her granddaughter then sat down, and asked her, "What do you notice?" She continued, "What difference do you notice between these three objects before and after they were cooked for 10 minutes?" Her granddaughter was very indifferent and told her that the differences were very obvious. She added, "Prior to being cooked for 10 minutes, the carrot was hard, rigid, and raw; whereas, after cooking the carrot, it became less rigid, softer, and flexible—with a sweet-smelling and lovely aroma." She continued, "On the other hand, the cooked egg is now solid, non-fragile, and will not easily break when compared to the raw, fragile, and liquid egg." Finally, she added, "The coffee is now cooked, liquid with a very beautiful aroma, and ready to be consumed; as opposed to the uncooked powder coffee—which is bitter and inconsumable in that state."

Now, If possible, I would like you to grab a pen and a sheet of paper and write down your thoughts about all the differences you could identify between each of these three objects before and after being cooked. Write down as many differences as you can possibly recognise. Now, what message or lesson can you draw from this story?

Of note, all three objects (the egg, carrot, and coffee) were subjected to the same conditions—the same containers (pots), the same amount of water, and the same temperature for the same amount of time. The heat/temperature in this case could be likened to the challenge that all three objects went through—which was the same. Nonetheless, the outcomes achieved subsequent to the challenge (cooking process) were quite different/unique to each object and based on their intrinsic nature and characteristics—and not on the challenge encountered (in this case, the heat).

"What you see and what you hear depends a great deal on where you are standing. It also depends on what sort of person you are." C.S. Lewis

In the same manner, when you go through challenges in life, it is usually of no benefit to focus on the challenge, magnify it, and/or start putting the blame on the challenging circumstances affecting or surrounding you. Furthermore, it is absolutely unnecessary to make reference to the magnitude of the challenge as the reason why you are very depressed, unable to find any solutions or are experiencing a lot of difficulties finding one. In essence, your focus and energy should be on you! Your perspective needs to change and move from the challenge to you—from the problem to the solution, as already discussed in great detail in the first chapter of this book.

Too often, a lot of people who do not cope well with managing challenges (or experience difficulties in effectively bouncing back after encountering some difficult life challenges) are very good at justifying why they seem to be in a poor, hopeless, and/or mediocre condition ... and often attribute this to the magnitude and gravity of the challenge they are undergoing or encountering. Notwithstanding, this is not the case and will never be the case. You should always remember that, just like the egg, coffee, and carrot, the outcomes achieved after you undergo/encounter great challenges or storms in life are closely correlated and linked to your personality and those intrinsic characteristics and qualities/values that shape and define you as an individual—and not to the external challenge or circumstances surrounding such a challenge.

Fundamentally, who you truly are – your core beliefs, values, thoughts, and attitudes – is grossly responsible for the way you deal with and overcome challenges in life. In reality, it is not the challenges that come your way in life that determine how you respond to them or who/what you become post-challenge. Rather, it is who you truly and authentically are and what you represent that will determine how you will respond to those challenges and who/what you become post-challenge.

I'm sure you would agree with me that it is very possible for two people to go through exactly the same challenge in life yet end up with two different and completely opposite responses and hence results/outcomes based on their personalities. Just like the carrot, egg, and coffee, having undergone exactly the same challenge not a single one of them came out the same as the other—with all three having completely different outcomes attributed to their intrinsic nature and characteristics.

"You can't always control circumstances. However, you can always control your attitude, approach, and response. Your options are to complain or to look ahead and figure out how to make the situation better." Tony Dungy

Another profound lesson to be drawn from this story that highlights the significance of changing your perception when confronted by adversities or life storms is this: just like the carrot, which was initially rigid/hard prior to the immersion in water and heating/cooking process but became softer/more flexible after going through the heating/cooking process or challenge, you may currently be very rigid/inflexible and hard on yourself and towards others.

65

Consequently, the challenge you are facing at the moment that seems unbearable has only come your way to accomplish a very unique purpose—that of making you more flexible and less rigid or sensitive towards yourself and your needs and expectations and towards others and their needs.

In the case of the egg, you might be very fragile and vulnerable in life or at this stage of your life, such that every single challenge or adversity you encounter in life causes you to break down—become stressed, anxious, and depressed. Hence, the purpose of what you are currently considering as a huge and unbearable challenge that has come to break and destroy you is simply a tool to strengthen and reinforce you and your core foundation. In effect, it is a timely device required to make you less fragile, unbreakable, and more resilient.

Finally, the amazing life lesson enveloped in the coffee is awesome and could be interpreted in your own life scenario as such: just like the coffee could never be consumed without being immersed and/or boiled in hot water – in addition to the fact that it has to be consumed together with the hot water and could not be separated from it – in the same way, some of the challenges/storms you perceive yourself to be currently going through in life are not necessarily life storms/challenges but requisites for the fulfilment of your purpose—and they must be regarded and embraced as such in order for you to fully exploit and maximise the benefits that come with them. That is to say, the purpose of the coffee could never be fulfilled without it going through the boiling process or perceived challenge. Just like gold would not be in existence in all its magnificence and splendor if it did not go through the furnace for the purification/refining process!

Now, my question to you is this: When you go through life challenges or storms, what are you like? Are you like an egg, a carrot or coffee? If given the opportunity to choose, which would you like to be like? Which is the best or the most resilient in nature? Of note, this is not a static point of reference but, rather, a very dynamic one. At different times or circumstances in your life, you may be one or more of these three, while in other times and circumstances, you could be another/a different one ... and that is very ok! Nonetheless, my most favourite of the three is the coffee. I so much love the coffee because it solidifies and buttresses the fact that you do not necessarily have to wait to come out of a challenging life situation or scenario (like what you may be currently going through at the moment while reading this book) before you can fully appreciate your worth and the beauty of who you are/represent and/or have become as a result of the challenge. Right there in the midst of the challenge/s, you could and should appreciate who you are – your authenticity, self-worth, and beauty – and be free and proud to be you.

In fact, you should and must have a great and positive attitude at all times – even in the midst of the challenge – feeling very optimistic and looking orward to embracing and overcoming the challenge and the next—with a profound and well-grounded knowledge of the fact that it is indispensable for the fulfilment of your purpose and that your true beauty, worth, and essence are destined to be revealed in that challenging situation.

"Change the way you look at things and the things you look at change." Wayne W. Dyer

Of note, every challenge or perceived challenge that comes your way in life, once embraced with optimism, comes to enrich you, make you grow, and become a more resilient and better person. Consequently, never let the storms of life change who you truly are—your inner beauty, core beliefs, values, thoughts, and strengths. Rather, let who you are equip and enable you with the power and desire to change and shape your circumstances to your advantage—with a deep knowledge and assurance of the fact that "all things work together for good to them that love God, to them who are called according to his purpose." Romans 8:28

Therefore, "Consider it pure joy, my brothers and sisters, whenever you face trials of many kinds, because you know that the testing of your faith produces perseverance. Let perseverance finish its work so that you may be mature and complete, not lacking anything." James 1:2–4

Also, you do not need to separate your past from the present or be ashamed of it, thinking it is horrible, shameful, and of no benefit to anyone at the moment. I can perfectly understand that; you might have had a horrible and shameful past you are absolutely not proud of—we all have made some wrong/misleading choices and decisions in the past we may not be proud of and wish we could change them. However, our mistakes and/or shameful past do not define us and will never do, unless we willfully or unwilling allow them to. They have been a very significant part of our journey to the present and must have pruned and shaped us in one way or another in becoming who we are today. You are a totality of your past, present, and future, and in this there is a great story to be told and numerous lives to be touched and impacted— it's all about your perception! What you may perceive as a mess could just be your ideal message of hope and encouragement to the world... It's all about how you perceive it.

"There are times in our lives when we have to realize our past is precisely what it is, and we cannot change it. But we can change the story we tell ourselves about it, and by doing that, we can change the future." Eleanor Brown

"The challenge is to draw on the past but not be bound by it." David Brazzeal

I would like to share with you another very emotional story I received from a friend through the internet. The story is so touching and full of real life lessons, especially for parents (regardless of whether it is a true story or not) with regards to their perceptions about their children's conduct.

Practically, what one parent will consider appalling and unacceptable behavior – deserving severe punishment – another may simply consider as a lack of love or attention/care on their part—and thus a cry for help and attention! Consequently, the latter will respond very differently and out of love and concern.

I heard about a young man who was polishing his new car, whilst his four-year-old son picked up a stone and scratched the side of the car. In anger, he took the child's hand and hit it many times—not realizing he was using a wrench! Following the incident, the child became very unwell and was rushed to the hospital. Whilst in the hospital, unfortunately, the child lost all of his fingers due to the multiple fractures he sustained as a result of the incident. When the child finally woke up and saw his father sitting by his bedside, with pain in his eyes he asked, "Dad, when will my fingers grow back?" The dad was so hurt and speechless; he sat there staring at his son with profound regret and remorse.

He later left the hospital and decided to take a walk back to his car... While there, he became even more frustrated and started kicking and punching the car. He kicked and punched the car several times with his head bowed! Devastated by his own actions, he sat down in front of the car weeping...

Suddenly, he lifted up his head and decided to take a second look at the scratches/dents that his son had made on the car and had the greatest shock of his life! He realised something he least expected—his son had scribbled these words boldly: "I LOVE YOU DAD." Immediately, his head dropped in anguish. With a heavy heart, he stood up and walked away from the hospital car park, leaving his car behind. The burden and consequences of his own actions were too heavy for him to carry, and it was told that the next day he committed suicide.

I would like you to take a moment to reflect on this story and how it may relate to your own life and family. If you are a parent, I will like you to think about this story the next time you are so frustrated and upset with your child/children because he/they have done something you consider unacceptable – or simply spilled some water or milk on the dinner table – after a difficult and stressful day at work.

Think first before you lose your calm and lash out at that child or your children. Too often we fail to recognise the fundamental difference between the child and the act. You must acknowledge that everyone makes mistakes (including you) and this is very ok as it provides room and the opportunity for learning and growth. However, the actions you take while in anger may have serious and even fatal consequences and implications that you will never be able to repair, amend, fix, or take back—therefore, beware!

Let's consider another example that is especially useful for parents, particularly those tasked with the responsibility of bringing up children in this 21st century technological era. Imagine you have a daughter who has been particularly naughty throughout the day and doesn't seem to listen to a single instruction from anyone, including you! Here you come again, this time instructing her to go downstairs, sit down, and eat her dinner. She goes downstairs to the dining room, sits down, stirs her food, and looks around, wondering and daydreaming. Then, two minutes later, she suddenly gets up from the table and runs upstairs towards you, screaming with much excitement in her voice,

"Mummy... Mummy... Mummy!" Now quite frustrated, you refuse to respond to her call and completely ignore her. Frustrated, but determined not to give up (as most children always do), she continues to approach you: "But... but ... Mummy ... please ... just a minute..." Yet, you continue to ignore her and walk away from her!

In an attempt to get your undivided attention, she screams even louder, jumping up and down with her hands reaching out for you... By now, you have lost it all. Suddenly, you start screaming at her and telling her off. "Be quiet now, stop shouting, and go back downstairs and finish your dinner... NOW!" You screeched so loud that you thought knots and bolts were loosening and falling off your head and you were almost losing your mind! Or maybe you are the type of parent who counts up to the number three, for action to be executed at the count of three, and so you add this routine to your instruction.

At this point, your very frustrated and disappointed daughter sadly and reluctantly heads for the dining table to finish off her dinner! Nonetheless, she is now upset, resentful, and maybe feeling unvalued, rejected, and lonely. There she sits, miserable and lonely, eating slowly and not actually enjoying her dinner ... in an attempt to please you. She continues eating and daydreaming when, suddenly, and purely out of despair, she accidentally spills her drinking water on the floor! Now she heads upstairs for you again one last time, only this time a little different. In a very low and disappointed voice, head bowed down (not even able to look at you in the eyes), she says, "Mum, I spilled—"

But before she can complete the sentence you lash out again. "What? Have you finished your dinner?"

Right now, she is sobbing and trying really hard to explain to you what happened. "Mum, I spilled my water!"

By now there is a greater adrenaline rush, and you lose it all again – this time even worse – and the situation escalates out of control. Now, only God alone knows what you would do or what could happen when, in reality, all your innocent and lonely little girl was looking for was your attention and company, your approval, love, and care! What a tragedy!

"Most misunderstandings in the world could be avoided if people would simply take the time to ask, 'What else could this mean?'" Shannon L. Alder

Now, all you need to do or always remember to do if the situation persists longer than five minutes (if you are one of those impatient parents) is to change your perception about the entire situation and adopt a new resolution strategy. Believe me, it works like magic! In addition, you will be able to save and strengthen your relationship with your daughter or son.

You could completely transform the entire scenario in a very positive way by simply taking a minute or so to reflect and think of it in these ways: "Maybe all she is trying to do is get my attention—I have been busy all day and not spent any quality and worthwhile time with her..." "Maybe she just needs to know that I love her and will always be there for her..." "Maybe she's had a difficult day in school and just wants a confidant to talk to and share her struggles with..." or "Maybe all she needs is a hug and cuddle from me..." and the list goes on and on—now shifting your attention and focus from the problem at hand towards a possible and peaceful resolution.

In a situation like this, what automatically happens is an unconscious spiritual, mental, emotional, and physical shift—you move from a position of being upset and aggressive to that of being calm and protective towards her/her needs. You move from a mindset of frustration to that of compassion and love for your daughter, from a position of judgement and condemnation to that of justification, compassion, and love. What a magnificent way to resolve a simple, yet complex problem—which if not addressed properly and in time may escalate and leave behind a huge wound that might be difficult to heal and needs much more time, resources, and interventions than originally required.

Now, let's consider one final example where you could effortlessly apply this strategy to bring about significant change/mind shift with tangible results and solutions to the problem or challenge at hand. I would like you to take a few minutes and imagine or visualise yourself currently being surrounded by friends who take absolute delight in constantly irritating you, putting you down, and humiliating you in front of everyone. They are constantly looking for every given opportunity to criticise, judge, and condemn you or talk ill about you. What would you do in a situation like this?

Once more, without you initially stepping aside to reflect and search deep/tap from within in order to gain in-depth knowledge and insights of who you truly are – your unique strengths and potential – it is impossible to respond to such a situation with wisdom, grace, and serenity. This is so because you cannot change them or their perceptions about you (unless they willfully choose to do so). They are the only ones capable of changing themselves/their perceptions. In effect, it is not your duty to try to change them and their perceptions about you—it is simply not your job or responsibility to try to get their approval!

On the other hand, what you could do, and have the power to do, is to change your perception and thoughts about them and the situation. You could very well ask me, "But how is this possible? How can I change my perception about them and a pathetic situation like this?" Again, I tell you it is quite simple and pretty much straightforward without any involvement of some sort of magical formulas or powers.

This is what I would highly recommend you to do: In the first instance, instead of getting all upset, frustrated, and depressed, the first and foremost advice I will give you is to change your perception about them! Change the way you now look at them. Do this with compassion and knowledge of the fact that they may have a problem of low self-esteem and confidence and think that by putting you down and constantly criticizing you it will make them look better than you and help them feel good about themselves. This may equally be a spouse who constantly puts you down and criticises you at every given opportunity. Would you spend all day in self-pity, feeling sad and lowly about yourself, or find the courage and power to just walk away from him/her and the environment with your head held high?

All you really need in a case like this is the serenity and mental strength to be able to accept the things you cannot change in life and to keep being who you truly are; while for such friends all you need is to show compassion or pity—in a case where they are not willing to change their attitude towards you. As a matter of fact, one thing you will notice with such people is that they are not just being mean and disrespectful to you alone but to everyone they come across or encounter in life. They are probably having deep self-esteem/confidence issues and being critical of everyone but themselves. Ultimately, you may need to walk away from such company, and in this simple way you have overcome and also have the serenity and peace of mind to move on.

Of course, the ultimate choice is yours and yours alone. Do not tell me you do not have a choice (as we often tend to think, assume, and hence believe in times when we are facing some very difficult and challenging moments in life and seem completely helpless and powerless). There is always a choice available to us, however painful that may sometimes be. For example, many people choose to keep on living and hoping for a better life despite their hardships and disappointments, yet others choose to take away their own lives by committing suicide and giving up every hope to live. On the other hand, making no decision is also a choice!

Happiness is a deliberate choice and decision as much as living and enjoying life beyond challenges. Joy, peace, patience, love, kindness, humility, and self-control are all fruits that stem forth from within—they are fruits of the spirit and have nothing to do with your surroundings or external circumstances and life challenges.

You could rightly and consciously choose to walk away from any negative and unhealthy situation/environment you find yourself in. But my question to you is this: What becomes of you after walking away from the situation and environment? How will this affect, mould, and shape you after walking away from the scene and from him/her or them? What would your self-esteem and confidence levels become after walking away?

Therefore, walking away as an only option and solution is not a good enough option/solution. Alternatively, and in a situation where walking away is neither an available option nor the ideal solution, you could simply choose to "shut your ears" and "stop your mind" from receiving such destructive and lifeless words—and start speaking to yourself the words that bring and give birth to life. You must speak words that authentically and genuinely describe you and that which you would love and want to hear and believe about yourself—and which your creator, who knows you better than anyone else on planet Earth, confirms and endorses! You could do this either by professing these words and affirmations inwardly to yourself/your mind, or aloud—whichever you feel more comfortable with. But you should note that the loudest and most persistent voice in your mind always prevails and wins!

Consequently, you must endeavour to fill your mind with positive and constructive thoughts and words at all times ... for as a man thinks, so he is. Your thoughts eventually become your words and actions/reality, whether you are conscious of this or not.

You will certainly discover that by simply changing your perception, the solution unfolds, leading to a peaceful resolution—either by courageously addressing the issue at hand with grace and serenity or courageously walking away from it with dignity and conviction into a place of rest, inner peace, and resolution. Now, take note that this decision has to be consciously and deliberately made by you—being convinced in your spirit that it is the ultimate choice and decision to make. No one can do this for you or compel you to do so.

You must be able to envisage the intangible, yet profound benefits and rewards you would reap from merely changing your perception from that of pessimism to that of optimism ... from being problem focused to solution focused ... before you will be able to do so. Nonetheless, as you read this book, my sincere hope and desire for you is that you may be able to get to this point or position of maturity and discernment sometime soon—if not now. In this way, you may be able to fully appreciate and enjoy all that life has got to offer you and give the very best of yourself to yourself, then to your spouse/family, friends, colleagues, community, and the world at large.

"No man has the right to dictate what other men should perceive, create or produce, but all should be encouraged to reveal themselves, their perceptions and emotions, and to build confidence in the creative spirit." Ansel Adams

In a case where you have changed your perception about the situation at hand, and embraced the best and most plausible perception, you still have not succeeded in resolving the problem; what you will need to do at this stage is proactively reflect on the questions set out below and authentically respond to them. Subsequently, you could move on to apply the next powerful strategy—which will be explored and outlined in the next chapter of this book. This strategy, which is centered on the power of focus, could now be easily implemented as a result of your current state of mind—which is results driven. Therefore, what you will now need to do amidst the persistent challenge and non-resolution is to focus all your energy and strength on the solution and the steps that create or will create such solution.

REFLECTION & ACTION PLAN

Now, I want you to imagine a very difficult situation you are currently experiencing or would dread to ever experience.

1. Write down two or more (maximum of three) ways in which you could view the problem.

    a. ....

    b. ....

    c. ....

2. Now, for each viewpoint, write down your reasons for adopting it.

    a. ....

    b. ....

    c. ....

    d. ....

    e. ....

    f. ....

3. Of the three or less viewpoints adopted, which of them creates less distress and unrest within you? Call this your "Golden View".

....

....

....

....

....

....

....

....

....

....

4. Why does this particular viewpoint (the Golden View) create less distress and unrest within you?

....

....

....

....

....

....

....

....

....

....

5. What could you do to implement the "Golden View" from now on until the problem is resolved or you experience total serenity and peace within?

....

....

....

....

....

....

....

....

....

....

Now write down this "GOLDEN VIEW" in bold, and say it out loud/repeat it each time a negative or pessimistic thought or perception about that challenging situation comes to your mind and stirs up anxiety/distress.

....

....

....

....

....

....

....

....

....

....

In doing this, you will be able to experience peace and serenity while staying optimistic and pressing on/forward. In the process, you also become more compassionate, loving, and forgiving ... being confident of the fact that everything happens for a reason, which will be unveiled with time.

Furthermore, it unlocks your awareness of the fact that you are in complete control of your emotions and thoughts and capable of making wise choices and decisions/staying positive and happy—whatever the situation or outcome.

"Most of us go through each day looking for what we saw yesterday and, not surprisingly, that is what we find."

James A. Kitchens

"Always remember, your focus determines your reality."

George Luca

CHAPTER THREE

The Power of Focus

"Keep your eyes on the finish line and not on the turmoil around you." Rihanna

There is incredible power in focusing. You could never underestimate the power of focus—it is one of our greatest and most priceless weapons for victory and success, especially when geared towards the right direction and channel. Too often, challenges are mere distractions that come our way to make us lose focus on our life goals and objectives and, hence, go off track. You must be mindful at all times, being aware of the great power that propels from a focused mind. Meanwhile, a distracted mind is rendered powerless and ineffective.

While growing up, I heard of so many amazing stories that elucidated the amazing transformational power of a focused mind from my dad. As a child, whenever I was distracted while doing my homework, my dad would lay so much emphasis on the fact that my degree of concentration was indispensable for my success then and in the future. He would then take the time to explain to me in more detail the importance and power of a focused mind. Sometimes, in order to elaborate and decipher how powerful a focused mind could be, Dad would use the example of how a magnifying glass is capable of setting a sheet of paper on fire, simply by bringing together the rays of the sunlight to focus on that sheet of paper—something otherwise impossible for the unfocused and dispersed sun rays to accomplish.

Consequently, a very good and almost perfect example that could always be used to highlight the power of focus is the sunlight. Imagine the rays of the sunlight shining on a sheet of paper all day long. Nothing actually happens to that sheet of paper as the sun rays are dispersed, which renders their collective intensity diffused and weakened. Notwithstanding, when these same rays are then brought together collectively to focus on that same sheet of paper, through the use of a magnifying lens, they are now capable of setting the sheet of paper on fire.

In the same way, in the midst of adversity, I urge you to focus all your strength, undivided attention, and energy, on the solution. Let your focus be on your ideal—on what you would like to see or experience out of your current situation or adversity. Your focus needs to be on all that you would rather have, be or do "in the now" or in the future in order to experience internal peace, joy, and fulfilment. Therefore, your undiluted and undivided attention should be on that which will take you and your energy/focus away from the current challenge/adversity you are facing or undergoing. Focusing on the former gives you a new energy and a new momentum to kick-start your journey towards victory and success... It births within you a new passion, energy, and desire for victory, inner strength, resilience, and peace.

"The powers of the mind are like the rays of the sun. When they are concentrated, they illumine." Swami *Vivekananda*

Remember, these strategies have to be deliberate—you need to consciously make the decision and choice that: "At this point and time, this is what I choose to do, and will do ... irrespective of what is happening around me or in my life." For this to be possible, your conscious mind needs to be activated at all times, until such a time when these strategies and techniques have now become a norm and need no effort to be activated and executed—which goes to affirm the famous saying that "Practice makes perfect."

Once this has become a norm, the conscious mind has no further role to play as there is no need for reason, analysis, logic, etc., and the information is handed over to the subconscious mind, which could be likened to some sort of a reservoir or storage compartment. Literally, the subconscious mind is where all that which is not needed or requiring the immediate attention of the conscious mind goes to for storage, to be used in times of immediate need or

94

significance—when there is insufficient time and resources to think effectively, reason, or analyse…

When we focus, this is literally what happens in our conscious mind: the object or solution we focus on is highlighted and brought to the attention of the conscious mind, which now becomes aware and receives the information for a solution as an instruction. It eventually goes to work—analysing and evaluating this information and seeking for every indication/clue that justifies or complements the instruction. In other words, it searches and brings together all other information that is similar to that particular instruction; it collects and attracts everything that looks similar to the desired ideal or that will bring about the desired solution. It then amplifies these signals/this information—providing compelling evidence for action and eventually executes it. In effect, like attracts like and repels unlike...

Consequently, when you have consciously trained yourself or your mind how to focus in order to produce outcomes and results that you desire to enable you to successfully resolve and overcome a specific issue or life challenge, your mind records that incident/episode as "memory" and stores it in your subconscious mind—as there is neither room nor need for it to remain in the conscious part of your mind. As a result, the next time you are faced with a similar adversity/life challenge, without a need for going through the entire synthetic process again, your subconscious mind then releases the stored information for your immediate and effective use, without any effort on your part. It works on your behalf to preserve and keep you safe and away from any preconceived threat or danger without questioning, analysing, judging, or justifying. This is the reason why, after you have done certain things in a certain way again and again, you do them automatically when confronted by a similar situation, and sometimes without even being aware or thinking!

We have heard people say again and again, "I just do it 'subconsciously'," or, more commonly, "unconsciously." Therefore, it will profit you at all times – especially in the midst of adversity or a difficult life challenge – to deliberately and consciously become aware of where your focus and energy lie. Because only in doing so will you be able to effectively take over control and manage the situation and your life—without letting it take control over you and manage your life.

In essence, where your focus consistently lies in the face of adversity will eventually determine the underlying foundational units and principles you build and establish to support and sustain you in times of adversity/crisis. These will eventually form those core subconscious beliefs, values, and principles on which basis you address and resolve similar and future life challenges, without any thoughts, analysis, judgement, or logic—which, in the long run, will form and represent your intrinsic problem-solving reservoir or bank.

At this stage, whether they are the right or wrong beliefs and hence right/wrong way to resolve the problem becomes irrelevant. In addition, whether you are aware of this or not is also irrelevant. All that is important and relevant is that this bank belongs to you, and all the resources therein are also yours (either directly deposited by you or indirectly by another with your consent), and it is therefore required to accomplish its purpose and role of supplying you with your deposits and resources in times of need and emergency.

Therefore, the only time and way you could contribute in ensuring that what is provided to you in times of genuine need is exactly what you need to resolve the situation at hand is at the time of your first/initial encounter with the given situation in consideration and by consciously intervening. You should and must know what your ideal is or would be at this very initial stage (which is the starting point). In other words, you must know what you want as knowing what you do not want – in this case, the adversity – does not guarantee knowing and having what you really want/need and success. It only guarantees the elimination of the unwanted/undesired and consequently creates a void, and, if the void is not filled, there will remain a continuous sense of unrest, un-satisfaction, wanting, and wandering... This is the reason why the first core and powerful strategy (reflection) for overcoming life challenges is paramount and critical in preparing you for the tasks and challenges ahead of you and comes in very handy at times.

If you are not quite sure of what your ideal is or looks like, I want you to simply take a minute, or the time you will need, to close your eyes... Now imagine and visualise what the solution would sound, look, feel, smell, or taste like... In other words, you should employ all of your possible physical senses to help you establish and experience what success will look, sound, smell, taste, or feel like. In it all, true success must always bring satisfaction, rest, inner peace, fulfilment, joy, and serenity. This is a simple guide to help you establish what ideals you should strive for – that will reflect and resonate the above traits/qualities – in case you are still confused and drowned in the situation and do not even know what the solution may look or feel like.

Now, having established what success means to you, the next step is to focus your undivided attention and all your energy on those things/resources that will create and bring about profound satisfaction, rest, inner peace, fulfilment, and serenity right in the very midst of the adversity or challenge. In so doing, you have made a conscious decision and choice of not only what you do not want or desire but also of what you truly desire/want and need and also consciously established the reason/s why you want or desire these outcomes—based on your knowledge of the fulfilment and satisfaction they will bring to you when accomplished.

Once this is very clear and settled in your conscious mind, there is really no longer any need for it to stay there, and it is now passed on to your "subconscious reservoir and bank". In a way, you have directly/indirectly influenced and controlled what currency/resources are saved up and stored in your subconscious bank—and available to be used in times of immediate need or an emergency. You have therefore deliberately deposited in your subconscious all the traits and qualities you would like exhibited when faced with a challenge—and unconsciously it will be required and prompted to release such in times of need. You will eventually reap what you sowed, and amazingly even more ... in abundance, as your mind will build up and amplify whatever information, solution or results you have created and deposited in it.

At this instant, I would like you to carry out a little exercise to further explore the power of focus. I would like you to be still wherever you are. If you are standing up and reading this book, that is perfectly fine, no need to change your position—remain standing. If you are lying down, remain lying, if you are sitting down, remain seated; all I am really interested in and requesting of you is your attention—your undivided attention, wherever you are right now. Look around and take note of every object that is coloured white. Now, start counting all the white objects you see around you, do this for about a minute. Then write down the number you arrived at, i.e. the total number of white objects you identified.

Now, I want you to look around and do the same again... What do you notice? Two things will be very evident here: firstly, your full attention is focused on finding only objects that are coloured white, in the midst of other coloured objects—and you will indeed find them. The actual amount of white objects you find the first time will depend on a number of factors (which I won't expatiate on as it is not very relevant to the exercise) including the actual amount of white objects found around you and your ability to effectively identify and single them out from the other objects in the given time frame.

Secondly, and interestingly, when you do this a second, third, fourth, or fifth time, you may be able to find more white objects (if there are actually more than you initially identified). Furthermore, the time taken to identify these objects will now reduce as your mind already has a recorded image and location of them and where they are respectively and is collecting and amplifying every signal that will enable it to accomplish the instruction of finding these white objects. Strangely and rightly so, you might not have noticed the other objects around you that are not white and/or close to the white objects you were interested in because your focus and goal was on finding only white objects.

Now, I would like you to do a similar exercise, but this time, your focus and goal should be on finding objects around you that are black. Now your conscious mind has been put to work and is collecting and bringing to your attention all those objects around you that are black while ignoring and/or eliminating every other object that is not black, as if they were not present within your surroundings! Does this mean there are now no white objects in the room or there were previously no black objects? Absolutely not! The only change is where your focus lay before and where it lies now—your focus has changed ... it has shifted from identifying and counting white objects to identifying and counting black objects.

If you are in the mood, you could now go on to identify and count every round object in your immediate surroundings, irrespective of what colour the objects are – your attention and focus should now be only on round objects – then, later on, the square ones, and so on and so forth... You would now be deliberately and consciously identifying and isolating objects, something you would not normally do if you were not instructed to do so and, hence, had not made the conscious and deliberate decision to do so. You could go on with this exercise and similar ones to help you bring the reality to light and also help you improve your ability to focus on solutions in the midst of challenge—and create the outcomes, results, and solutions you desire and set for yourself.

Another perfect example to elucidate the role and the power of focus in bringing about solutions is to look at the process of buying a new car. Have you ever noticed what happens whenever you are about to buy a new car? Have you realised that immediately after you have made the conscious decision about the specific type of car you would like to purchase, and resolved or settled in your conscious mind the reasons why you would like to have that particular type of car (and not another), you suddenly seem to see that particular car everywhere you drive or go? What has suddenly happened? Where have these cars been all the while that you couldn't see them? Has "The Universe" suddenly decided to throw more of such cars at you—and everywhere you go? Absolutely not! They have always been and will always be there, it's just that you have never noticed them before as you were focusing on several other things every time you drove—except for that particular brand or make of car. Your focus was elsewhere... Now your focus in on these types of cars and your mind is put to work—finding and attracting every single car that has your specifications and bringing them to your attention to create a response and solution to your appeal.

This is exactly what happens in a real-life scenario when you encounter challenges and you choose to move your focus from the problem in front of you to the results and solutions that you want to create and experience... You automatically start seeing and attracting not only all the things that represent the solutions you yearn for and are looking for but, interestingly, only those things that are similar and look like the solutions! Therefore, by default, you ignore and exclude all other things around you, including the problem itself and your ability to reason and judge otherwise. All you now see is the desired outcome/solution, and the pathway or various pathways that may lead to such a solution. The latter greatly motivates you and births a new energy and desire/momentum within you to start taking those initial steps and eventually maintaining the necessary steps that will help take you closer to the pathway/s and/or solution/s.

Beware! Your ability to focus alone wouldn't solve the problem or create the solution. Nonetheless, it will act as some sort of a catalyst that will help speed up the process to get you back on track from the deviation—back on track to achieving your goals and objectives you had set for yourself prior to the challenging encounter. Just like those cars that keep appearing in front of you or by you each time you drive, if you do not make the decision to act – by saving up money for the purchase and, most importantly, by practically going out there and purchasing the car – then you will never be able to own it. Regardless of how much you focus all your strength and undivided attention on it, it will remain a mere wish or dream and never become a reality.

"Until accompanied by an action, your goals are mere wishes and dreams."

Dr Sylvia Forchap-Likambi

Furthermore, if nothing is ever done to move you closer to acquiring the car, then it will eventually become an illusion ... and I guess you do not want to live your life this way. The truth is you can achieve, and are capable of achieving, all that you set your heart, mind, and strength on achieving. I guarantee you this, my friend, if only you believe and have faith you can achieve all your ideals and overcome whatever challenge you are faced with in life, with grace and serenity. Yet faith alone without works is insufficient. Your faith must be backed up with actions—for faith without works is death (James 2:20). This now takes us to the next and fourth powerful strategy needed to overcome challenges and adversities and live a happy and fulfilled life—which is The Power of Action.

REFLECTION AND ACTION POINTS

The purpose of this section is to provide you with the opportunity to fully reflect on the preceding strategy, which is the power of focus, then test and validate it— by effectively applying it and those principles learned from the chapter in your own life when faced with adversity or a challenging life situation.

I would like you to take some time to genuinely reflect on the following questions and answer them when faced with any given life challenge. The challenges may differ, yet the fundamental and underlying principles required to resolve them remain the same. So, whatever it is you are going through in your life right now (whatever it is that is really bothering you and causing continuous stress and unrest in your life) I would like you to take note of it—acknowledge it and then write it down, to the best of your ability.

Remember, this is not a test, and there is no right or wrong answer—they are simply the adversities and challenging situations in your life, identified and acknowledged by you. What we need to achieve here is to get you into a place of consciousness—into a place where you consciously and deliberately make the choice to walk towards the path that will find and create a solution to your problem/s, as opposed to just staying or sitting there and focusing on the problem and asking, "But why me?"

Now ask yourself these questions and reflect on them to find the answers that will bring clarity of mind and focus:

1.   Why am I here? Or what am I doing here in the first place?

....

....

....

....

....

....

....

....

....

....

....

....

2.   Where am I going to?

....
....
....
....
....
....
....
....
....
....

3.   What is my final and ideal destination?

....
....
....
....
....
....
....
....
....
....

4. When do I hope to get to this destination?

....
....
....
....
....
....
....
....
....
....

5. What will I do when I get there?

....
....
....
....
....
....
....
....
....
....

6. Why will I do that?

....

....

....

....

....

....

....

....

....

....

7. How will I feel?

....

....

....

....

....

....

....

....

....

....

8. Now, how can I get there?

....

....

....

....

....

....

....

....

....

....

9. What path or pathways must I take now? Or what can I
    do right here and now to start my journey towards my
    ideal destination?

....

....

....

....

....

....

....

....

....

....

Now, being assured of the reason why you find yourself where you are at the moment, where you are going to, why, and how you will feel when you get there and do this helps you focus on your destination and stay on track and not be derailed or distracted by the challenges/adversities in your life. In effect, your answers to the above questions will help you outline and establish your main life goals and purpose— and therefore give you the ultimate reasons why you shouldn't be distracted or give up but rather stay focused and persist until your goal/purpose is accomplished.

"The future depends on what you do today." Mahatma Gandhi

"It's the action, not the fruit of the action, that's important. You have to do the right thing. It may not be in your power, may not be in your time, that there'll be any fruit. But that doesn't mean you stop doing the right thing. You may never know what results come from your action. But if you do nothing, there will be no result." Mahatma Gandhi

CHAPTER FOUR

The Power of Action

"Action may not always bring happiness, but there is no happiness without action." William James

"Every action geared towards the solution and final destination is worthy, and deserves recognition and acknowledgement." Dr Sylvia Forchap-Likambi

Never underestimate the significance of a single step in a journey of a thousand miles nor a simple word or sentence in the process of writing and publishing a book. Every action geared towards the solution and final destination is worthy and deserves recognition and acknowledgement. You would never become a millionaire, for instance, if you

115

lacked just one penny to round up the figure to a million. Furthermore, every journey of a thousand miles begins with a single mile/step...so just do something about that situation, NOW—whatever it is that will take you a step closer to the solution... Just do it!

One of the things that often hold people back and prevent them from acting is their continuous search for that which they need/do not have, or lack, in order to act. When your focus is on the things or resources that you do not have or would need in order to take action, it is very difficult to act—hence, frustration and anxiety step in, and you appear helpless and unable to take full control or even partial control of the situation at hand. My advice to everyone who finds himself/herself in such a situation is always the same— in order to act without giving it a second thought, you must channel your focus to what you have at hand ... what you have or are in possession of in the here and now to help bring about the solution. In other words, ask yourself this question: "What have I got in my hands?" Just like God asked Moses in Exodus. Too often in life, the resources we need to resolve and overcome our daily life challenges or adversities are right within us and/or within reach. Yet, we often look away from us and sometimes too far—in search of that which we already possess.

Now, before you start thinking, *I may need new skills to be able to resolve and overcome this problem,* my question to you is this: what skills do you already possess? What strengths do you already have? Focus on your strengths, exploit and maximize them to the fullest—this type of mindset will greatly motivate/energize you to keep going and pressing on in your endeavour to resolve the problem and challenge. You need to become aware of the fact that motivation is the process that initiates, guides, and maintains goal-oriented behaviours—in other words, solution-focused behaviours.

Energy is a key component that is vital in order to kick-start the journey—and hence the initiation of the motivation process. Such energy could be defined as potential energy—which is unused/stored energy in an object (the unused strength, talent, and ability that reside within you). In physics, potential energy, expressed in science as U, is defined as energy that is stored within an object, not in motion but capable of becoming active.

When at rest, every object (including you and me) has rest mass—the usual inertial (tendency to resist an applied force and movement). Once movement begins, resistance is overcome, and potential energy is then converted into kinetic energy (moving energy), which is energy possessed by an object in motion. In other words, when you remain still and make no effort whatsoever to move or take action, nothing happens—even the forces of nature at your disposal cannot help you. On the contrary, when you take action, you move from a state of dormant/stored energy and untapped potential to a state of active energy and acquire the strength that is needed to kick-start the whole process of your journey.

You might have reflected for a long time and came out with the best possible solutions and pathways ever; you might have also changed your perception and embraced the best and most optimistic perception ever – THE GOLDEN VIEW – and focused all your undivided and undiluted resources, strength, energy, and potential on the most satisfactory outcomes and solutions desired; yet, if you do not take the necessary actions or steps required to move towards that pathway and solutions/outcomes ... nothing will change! In effect, you will never be able to achieve such desired results and outcomes!

Just as an object while at rest has inertia (the tendency to resist an applied force and movement), you are also more likely to resist an applied force to move you, until you start moving. Of note, the law of inertia states that an object at rest will remain at rest and resist any motion unless an external force causes it to move, while an object in motion will keep moving in the same direction of motion and at the same momentum until an external force causes it to change direction or move faster.

Consequently, all that you really need to do is just start. Do not worry about how you will achieve the bigger picture. Once you kick-start the resolution process, every other thing will eventually fall into place – either to bring about a change in your situation or a change in you – such that you will be able to experience a sense of peace and serenity. Furthermore, once you start acting, you become less anxious or, even better, you are no longer anxious or stressed, nor do you worry any longer. Your brain/mind is at rest. Your brain becomes aware of the fact that action has been taken in response to the signal/situation at hand and therefore gives positive feedback—which fuels you with more energy and the strength to keep going and stay on track until the problem is resolved or a solution is reached. In the subsequent paragraphs, I will take some time to discuss in detail what actually goes on within us whenever we take action in response to a challenging or stressful situation.

On encountering a specific life challenge, you may feel stressed, but this is good news. Stress is a physiological condition that occurs when your body responds to external/internal stimulants to protect you—either by taking you away from the stimulant/perceived danger (when you do not possess the ability and capacity to fight the battle or affront the challenge) or by enabling you to fight, overcome, and conquer the battle/perceived danger or challenge you are faced with. As part of this process, and in order to provide you with the much-needed strength and energy that you would not initially possess in your dormant/undisturbed and laid-back state, or to enable you to fully exploit the stored/unused energy and potential within you, adrenaline, cortisol, dopamine, and other stress-related hormones are being released.

These hormones enable your heartbeat to increase, your muscles to contract faster, etc. so as to enable you to engage in the "Fight or Flight" process of a physiological battle. At this stage, you are well equipped and capable of taking further action. Once the action has been taken, these chemicals/stress hormones are then reabsorbed. Your brain becomes aware of the fact that the threat/problem is being dealt with or taken off. Consequently, there is no longer any reason or need to amplify the signal—and positive feedback is provided. The latter then enables you to relax and rest/be at peace.

Nonetheless, stress becomes pathological when it persists longer than it should. Irrespective of whether or not the problem/established threat is real or only perceived as real, your brain still sees it as a threat to you. As a result, it keeps working to produce more of these stressors/stress hormones to rescue you from the threat/perceived threat. Over time, you accumulate more chemicals – cortisol, adrenaline, etc. – than needed for the body to function appropriately, and the re-uptake and/or breakdown mechanisms do not have sufficient time to either take up or break down the excess hormones/chemicals that are being produced at a rapid rate. Consequently, you now find yourself in a situation where you have chronic stress and eventually depression (which in very simple terms is the reflection of an imbalance in chemicals within your brain).

Of note, emotions are simply messages to your brain instructing it to take action in order to take you away from danger and to preserve/protect you. If no action is taken, the messages/messengers and chemical release are amplified, leading to chronic stress—which may eventually lead to anxiety (as you tend to worry and feel helpless, unable to manage and/or control the situation) and depression (as a result of the chemical imbalances within your system and body). Such chemical imbalances eventually affect your other organs, too, resulting in further complications and making you more unwell.

I'd like us to now consider a very simple and practical example that may help you better understand

and embrace how this seemingly complex principle and mechanism works. This straightforward example will also enable me to elucidate the significance of taking actions when stressed or overwhelmed with challenging life situations (irrespective of how minimal or insignificant the action may seem).

Imagine you are very hungry and have not eaten anything in the last eight hours. When you are hungry, this is literally what happens: the feeling of hunger, which is an emotion (message), is transmitted as signals to your brain— notifying it of your current state of hunger and the need for action. Basically, it instructs your brain to do something in order to feed your cells and body and keep them functioning properly. Precisely, a message is sent to your brain notifying it that you are very hungry and need to eat now. This message is then picked up by the brain cells as a signal and amplified—so it becomes very evident and obvious to every cell and organ around your brain and your entire body as well. The subsequent process then solicits the attention and collaboration of all the other cells and organs required to bring about the best physiological solution ever—which is that of providing nutrients and nourishment to your body.

I will not get into the details of all the chemical and physiological processes involved here as they are not very relevant for the purpose of this book. However, what I want to place emphasis on and bring to your attention is this: if no action is taken to resolve the issue of hunger, or no solution is reached, the signal of hunger will not go away. Conversely, it will be further amplified—more chemicals/stressors will be released, resulting in physiological/pathological conditions like blood vessel dilation, increase in heart rate, headache, intestinal muscle contraction or spasm/cramp—and it may eventually result in far worst conditions if you still do not eat and the signal persists.

Now, let's envisage a case where your brain receives this signal or message of hunger and transmits/translates it to you as a need for food or to eat—and you immediately take action. Imagine you go grab something to eat and eventually sit down to eat. Do you realise that as soon as you take in the first mouthful of the food, even though you haven't yet finished the entire meal and are not yet satisfied, your body chemistry instantly changes? You are like, "Wow! How delicious! Mmm..." You feel more relaxed, less frustrated, and gradually begin to feel a sense of satisfaction as you continue to eat—even though you still need to eat more before you can be fully satisfied. This is possible because your mind (or, more appropriately, your brain) receives feedback that action is currently being taken by you and there is no longer need for any further action or stress hormones to be released.

At this stage, you then transmit a different signal—that of satisfaction, fulfilment, and resolution. In addition, your system ensures that all chemicals initially released are either broken down and eliminated or taken up for storage until needed next—resulting in an overall sense of satisfaction and relaxation. Of note, when you finally sit down to eat, you do not and cannot put all of the food into your mouth in one go in order to enable you to achieve complete satisfaction. You take it one mouthful and one bite at a time. You keep doing this until you are satisfied and no longer hungry.

This is exactly what happens when you are faced with a challenging situation in life—as soon as you start taking action (no matter how small it may be), even if it is just a single step towards resolving the bigger picture or problem, all the feelings of anxiety, worry, helplessness, and stress, gradually and eventually fade away. Sometimes the step may just be as simple as taking out more time to be still, reflect, and meditate—in search of inner wisdom and guidance. Other times it may be as simple as exercising patience; showing love; care; asking for forgiveness; forgiving another; giving or receiving a hug … and so on. On the other hand, as long as you do not take action, the situation persists and worsens.

Looking back at some of the previous examples we considered earlier in this book, such as the case of "that daughter of yours", who needed your attention and care. In this case, the initial and maybe only action to be taken could be as simple as having an honest and open one-to-one conversation with her; hugging her and reassuring her of your unconditional love for her; or simply listening to her with your undivided attention. While in the case of the very critical and judgemental friend or spouse, it could be a simple action like ignoring them and making the decision to walk away—

while encouraging and reminding yourself of how wonderful and glorious you are as an individual and a friend/ spouse.

"Action expresses priorities." Mahatma Gandhi

At this instant, while taking a step at a time, you might not have arrived at your final destination yet or fully resolved the challenge at hand, but not withstanding, all that is needed is to keep going, keep pressing on, and acknowledging where you have come from, how far you have come, where you are at the moment, and celebrating those seemingly little steps of progress and milestones achieved thus far. Each action fuels you with energy and momentum—providing you with more strength/force and the motivation and drive to carry on and not give in or quit.

Furthermore, by recognising and acknowledging those milestones, you open the door to many more opportunities. Also, this is an indication that you are fully aware and conscious of what happened, where you were, how far you have come, what is currently going on, and the pathway and direction you have chosen and navigated so far. All of the above states of consciousness result in you being more relaxed, calm, and serene. These emotions could also be validated and explained physiologically as resulting from the reuptake/elimination of the stressors and the release of relaxants or hormones that bring about relaxation—such as the popular "feel good hormone", endorphin.

Remember that action is a doing thing, it is not a thinking or talking thing ... therefore, just do it now! Act now! Not later, not tomorrow, not in a week's time, but now!

REFLECTION AND ACTION POINTS

Now, after reading the previous chapter, which unveiled the fourth powerful strategy to implement in overcoming life challenges—which is the power of action, I would like you to take some time and reflect on the following questions as a guard to support you in testing and immediately applying this strategy straightaway in your life. Take as much time as you may require, reflect on the questions and on your answers, and eventually apply them in your life—where and when relevant.

Consequently, I want you to ask yourself the following questions and write down your answers here using the first person singular to refer to yourself, thus making it very personal.

1.   What possible action/s could I take now that will move me a step closer towards the desired solution to my problem or challenge?

....

....

....

....

....

....

....

....

....

....

2.   Is there any other thing I could do here and now while waiting for the solution to unfold? If yes, what can I do? If no, why?

....

....

....

....

....

....

....

....

....

....

3. What little/baby steps could I take today and every other day to get me at least a step closer to my desired destination? Or what could I do now to take me a step closer to my destination?

....
....
....
....
....
....
....
....
....
....

4. What are the other steps or things that I could do to help me arrive at the solution?

....
....
....
....
....
....

....

....

....

....

Now write down in any order (as they come to your attention) all the possible steps or actions you can think of that would take you closer to your goal/final destination.

....

....

....

....

....

....

....

....

....

....

Once you have written down all of the required steps and actions you would need to undertake in order to achieve the solution, or get you closer to your final destination, I want you to number or regroup them in terms of priority and significance—by allocating numbers to them, beginning with the number one for the first step or action point of greater significance to be taken.

5.   Next, take the first three priority action points and allocate a time limit after each one of them, in order of priority. At this stage, ensure that you personalise each of the action points or steps. Below is an example of how best you could write it:

I will do...today, the........... (Include the date of today) by 8:00 p.m. tonight. Or in a much more compelling format: I must do......................................by 8:00 p.m. tonight (Make sure you take the action/step immediately ... now, not tomorrow, not next week, not next month, not next year ... but now!

....

....

....

....

....

....

....

....

....

....

6. Do I need any help with what I am doing? If yes, what
    help do I need? From where?

....

....

....

....

....

....

....

....

....

....

From who? And when do I need this help?

....

....

....

....

....

....

....

....

....

....

What else can I do later on that will move me towards my goal/the desired solution?

....

....

....

....

....

....

....

....

....

....

Now write all the other ideas that may help you move closer to the solution and enable you to overcome the challenge. Write them down as they come to your mind and in no particular order:

....

....

....

....

....

....

....

....

....

....

Now, looking at all the possible steps/actions you have just written that, if taken, would potentially lead you towards the solution, I want you to assign numbers to each action point in order of priority (similarly to what you did before). In other words, regroup and/or reorder them now by assigning numbers and then timescales by the side of each action point. This will enable you to come up with a list of solution-focused activities—thus shifting your attention and focus from the problem to your list of possibilities and opportunities needed to resolve the challenge or problem at hand. Such attitude will fuel you with more energy, enthusiasm, and optimism to keep going and pressing on.

Every step of the way, never forget to acknowledge where you have come from and the small, yet progressive steps and strides you have taken thus far. Be grateful for every given opportunity to progress and while progressing. Also, remember to always show gratitude to all those who help you along the way and for the grace and strength to carry on.

"Let gratitude be the pillow upon which you kneel to say your nightly prayer. And let faith be the bridge you build to overcome evil and welcome good."

Maya Angelou

"Gratitude can transform common days into thanksgivings, turn routine jobs into joy and change ordinary opportunities into blessings."

William Arthur Ward

CHAPTER FIVE

The Power of Gratitude

"Gratitude unlocks the fullness of life. It turns what we have into enough, and more. It turns denial into acceptance, chaos to order, confusion to clarity. It can turn a meal into a feast, a house into a home, a stranger into a friend. Gratitude makes sense of our past, brings peace for today and creates a vision for tomorrow." Melody Beattie

"Never let a day go by without looking for at least one thing in your life to be happy and grateful for...there will be hundreds of reasons to be grateful, if your focus is on finding them." Dr Sylvia Forchap-Likambi

Gratitude is a powerful and very fulfilling attitude and life experience. The more grateful you are in life, the more fulfilled/satisfied and happy you are with your life and the surrounding circumstances. This is so because you tend to focus on the things you already possess or are sure of possessing, which implies your focus is not on what you don't have or need, but rather it is on what you already have or you are certain you will have. When you do this very often, there is no room for wanting, regret, ingratitude, or worry. On the contrary, you constantly find yourself in a position of satisfaction, abundance, acknowledgement, and appreciation of life—regardless of other obvious challenges or obstacles you may be facing in life.

"A cheerful heart is good medicine, but a broken spirit saps a person's strength." Proverbs 17:22

Consequently, as you continue towards your journey of gradually overcoming the challenges/adversities you are faced with, it is fundamental and highly therapeutic that you exhibit an attitude of gratitude. Be grateful for the opportunity presented to you for change; be grateful for each new day; be grateful for each step encountered and overcome—even for the ones still to be encountered and overcome. Be thankful for the fact that you are still alive—for good health ... as some might not have survived the situation you are currently going through, while others' health might have completely deteriorated if faced with a similar situation or challenge.

"Be thankful for what you have; you'll end up having more. If you concentrate on what you don't have, you will never, ever have enough." Oprah Winfrey

Be thankful at all times, regardless of what the situation might be. At the very least, it is not over yet and you are given another chance to make it right again—maybe two, three, four, or five more chances ... you may never know. As long as you are alive, then there is still hope for you—the battle is not over yet, and you are not a victim but a victor. Be thankful for the fact that the current situation has not consumed and drowned you—you are still swimming in the ocean of adversity. Yes you are, surely and steadily, to the shore of rest and resolution—still sane, or half sane, and free.

At the least, you are not locked up in some sort of a prison or psychiatric ward (even if you are you are still alive, and therefore there is hope for you too). Change is still possible—it is the only one thing in life that is constant and guaranteed and happens all the time by the seconds, minutes, hours, days, weeks, months, and years. Therefore, if you are reading this book while you or a loved one of yours is currently in prison or in a psychiatric home, do not be discouraged or give up just yet—there is still immense hope for you and/or your loved one. Be thankful for the priceless gift of life itself—for where there is life there is also hope. Only the living can bring hope. Again be thankful for another unique opportunity to settle scores and make it right again. In the case of that "beautiful daughter of yours", thank God for another opportunity to be able to reconnect with her and love her again.

On the other hand, is the challenge you are facing right now got to do with your health? Is it about your weight? Whatever it may be, no one is undermining it and neither should you undermine it, nor have to justify to anyone why you feel the way you do about the situation. Your feelings/emotions, perceptions, and thoughts are valid— whatever they may be.

I will tell you about a very recent incident that happened to me and how consciously adopting and implementing an attitude of gratitude greatly transformed the entire situation and made it an experience worth living/very fulfilling and productive—amidst the challenges that preceded the circumstances.

Recently, we had booked a return journey to Dublin, Ireland, for a family vacation. We were supposed to travel by air very early in the morning for our outbound journey (which was a 55-minute journey) so we would have enough time to pick up our hired car, drive to our hotel, check in, explore the city, and rest. Unfortunately, due to some unforeseen circumstances and inappropriate planning, we finally arrived at our departure gate a minute after the final boarding call was made ... only to be told our plane was ready for takeoff and the gate was now closed—so they could no longer board us! We were absolutely devastated! If you have ever travelled with three young children, including a one-year-old baby then you will understand the logistics involved when travelling with young ones by air! It had been a long and stressful process from arrival to check-in/security checks, etc. only to finally arrive at the gate to be told we had missed our flight and couldn't travel!

My husband and I were so upset, while our daughter and son thought it was funny—that is the beauty and innocence of children. We were then told we would have to take the next flight, which was due in four hours, and were escorted by the security team through another route to the main departure terminal for a complete start over again!

My husband (whose default position is always to blame me for any lateness) immediately entered into his default position, in spite of all that I had been doing/done to facilitate our early departure and arrival! To my astonishment, he immediately kick-started his default blame mood, which I couldn't really bear or take in. As a result, and out of frustration, I also lashed out, refusing to take the blame and pointing out very firmly that it was a joint responsibility—and if we had planned properly, collaborated, and worked as a team, then the end result would have been completely different. We would never have missed the flight nor arrived late at the airport to start with. But being who he is – with a very strong conviction about his opinions – he wouldn't admit anything different, let alone take responsibility for having contributed to the incident. He even lashed out at the kids as well, blaming them for the delay and incidence! To me, this was absolutely wrong and unacceptable as it is our key responsibility as parents to ensure they wake up on time and be on time. As much as we must train them to become responsible, yet, we cannot blame them for a collective action we needed to take to ensure things were intact.

Our differences in opinion, coupled with our disappointment and frustrations, led to a heated argument, which was absolutely uncalled for! At one point I had to decisively and quickly take the opportunity to focus on the first powerful strategy outlined in this book (reflection and silence) to help me overcome the challenging situation I was then faced with. I immediately and consciously decided to channel my energy and focus within rather than outward and reflect on the situation, but with a focus on the solution rather than the problem itself.

While I reflected, my husband immediately said we were no longer travelling and had to return home—so this could serve as a life lesson to us all, excluding him, of course! I tried to explain to him as calmly as possible about the implications and great financial loss we would incur for making such a negative and emotional decision.

Now back at the departure desk, I went on to enquire about the time and cost of the next flight to Dublin. To my greatest surprise and disappointment, the flight that was due in four hours was fully booked, making it practically impossible for us to depart within the next four hours. The only option given to us was to wait for the subsequent flight, which still had some availability and was due in 11 hours! I stood there astounded yet determined not to give up but to find a solution. Now, with a solution-focused mindset, I suddenly remembered that it was possible to also travel to Dublin via the train/ ferry line—and this created a spark of hope and determination again within me.

I was then ushered to the information desk, where I could get all the relevant information I needed to go Dublin from Liverpool on the same day. In all this, I deliberately decided not to approach my husband (who was apparently waiting for me to join him so we could go back home) and to avoid any sort of futile and unproductive communication with him. I was determined to change my perception about the entire incident and remain optimistic. I was not ready for any cynical comments or pessimism as these would have been quite draining and discouraging.

To cut a long story short, I decided to make a very deliberate and conscious decision—that, irrespective of all the ups and downs, I was going to remain grateful and focus on all the reasons and things I had to be grateful for—and there were quite a lot! I started off expressing gratitude for being alive and having amazing health then for having a second chance to make it right—for another opportunity to still travel to Dublin earlier on that same day.

Everything was eventually sorted out, and we were scheduled to take the next train from Liverpool within an hour from then, so we could be able to board the ferry to Dublin, which was due to depart within the next five hours. While on the train and ferry, I had much time to ponder and reflect again on all the amazing things and opportunities I should be grateful for.

Finally, on arrival at Dublin, I was so grateful for journey mercies and for the beautiful scenery. I was very grateful that we had finally made it in the end and did not lose everything. I was grateful for the awesome and fabulous quality family time away from every other distraction. In effect, I decided that I was going to make it the best vacation in my life so far! In fact, I became so self-aware and conscious that every moment of my vacation was centered on gratitude and making the best of it. I immediately stopped talking about the past.. and began living in the moment and enjoying every single moment the best I could.

I spent a considerable amount of time also reflecting on my life and how I could consistently work on developing myself and living and enjoying life to the fullest—with no regrets whatsoever! At the end of the vacation, I was greatly refreshed, re-energised and restored! Indeed, it was one of my best and quality vacations ever.

I have literally observed and experienced the power of gratitude work miracles both in the lives of close friends and loved ones and in my life. Gratitude provides you with more fuel and the strength to carry on—to sustain the journey, the healing and restoration process.

Regrets will literally rob you of appreciating the amazing little and precious/priceless things and moments in your life. They will rob you of living in the present and experiencing the many blessings and opportunities that it brings and holds. Therefore, do all in your ability to consciously choose a guilt-free life with no regrets over a life full of guilt and regrets.

A life of guilt and regret will rob you of your joy and inner peace. Regretting does not and will never help you resolve a problem or overcome a challenge in life. It will never make you feel any better or even good, so why waste your valuable time and life regretting? Live and experience the present with a heart full of joy and gratitude.

In the second part of this chapter, I would like to share with you another story that uncovers the miraculous power entrapped in gratitude. This happened two years ago, when I was planning to launch one of my new ventures. There was a lot of pressure on my team and me to get everything sorted and ready on time so as to meet the deadline of the launch. Part of the main problem that held us back was the fact that we did not gain access to our new premises on the expected and scheduled date, due to some delays on the part of the previous tenants. This delay caused us huge setbacks with regards to the timescale allocated for refurbishment and decoration of the premises prior to the launch. No one was available to execute the work within 48 hours of the launch at such short notice.

Even though we were amateurs when it came to painting/decoration work, we collectively agreed as a team to take up the task, in addition to other workloads we had. In the course of initiating the work, I realised we were doing more damage than good and making the venue look more unattractive than it was prior to the start of our work. At this, I hesitantly told my colleague who was the lead, and determined to learn as we progressed (and who was by now very stressed and almost covered with paint), that I was profoundly grateful for his commitment and dedication but I didn't think this was a good idea. I told him it would be a good idea to stop the work, clean ourselves up, and the room we were currently painting, and try to get a professional to do the job.

He was not very happy with this decision and became even more stressed. His temperament and body language were not very helpful at a time like this. In all honesty and sincerity, I thanked him for his loyalty and dedication and assured him I fully understood how stressful and urgent the situation was and that I took full responsibility for this and I was doing everything possible to make it right and less stressful for the team—in the best possible way I could. I went further to tell him that, at this point in time, we needed more positive energy and strength than ever before and this could only stem from within us.

On the other hand, I got him to understand that being in a negative and pessimistic mood and environment was futile and detrimental. I then assured him that it was ok for him to take a break and go home to rest and unwind and be back the next day. At that point in time, I did not need any form of negativity around me, especially as I had only just recently found out that I was about 10 weeks pregnant with my third child! I was somehow physically frail and suffering from morning sickness and needed to preserve every form of positive energy I possibly could to keep me mentally, emotionally, and physically strong and fit.

I also reminded my colleague that just as positivity is contagious, so too is negativity—and, even worse, as it saps the energy out of us. We then carried on to clean and tidy up the mess we had made. I kept singing songs of praise and thanksgiving, and being especially thankful for everything that had gone well so far, as I continued to work. I was thankful for the premises, thankful for the new venture, for the amazing and supportive staff I had, and above all for the grace and gift of optimism, serenity, and tenacity—amidst all odds. This attitude of mine gave me a deep sense of reassurance and confidence that everything would be fine.

In the meantime, I browsed through my contacts in search of any builder or painter I could get hold of at such short notice. While I did this, one of my colleagues and the caterer for the launch walked into the building to do some decoration work in the area where she was going to be serving the buffet. I realised that she had also come in with some paint and I asked her if she could paint. Immediately she told me no but that her uncle, who was behind her, was a professional painter and was going to help her!

Another light bulb moment! I lit up with a very bright smile and joy within me and immediately turned to her uncle and asked with a massive smile on my face, "Could you please help us do some decoration work here? We are stuck and almost stranded. Please," I continued with an even brighter smile this time. "Could you help us, please? We need it done within 48 hours!" I added.

He smiled at me and said, "Yes I can. Show me around, so I can see all the work that needs to be done," he added.

By now, I was screaming and jumping like a toddler who had just been given his favourite toy and saying, "Thank you! Thank you! Thank you very much!" We then discussed the costs, and it was a pretty good offer too! That was one problem out of the way, and I was forever so grateful and optimistic. Besides, my colleague was now smiling as well...

The next problem we had was getting our service brochure printed and delivered to us on time for the launch!

There had been some major incompatibility problems with our original design that was sent for print in respect to the printing specifications and guidelines. Our designer was not immediately available to resolve this problem when it was first identified and brought to our attention. This meant that we incurred further delays. However, when the designer became available, he immediately got in touch with the printing agency staff and started liaising with them to get the brochure in the correct format requested. They copied me in on all email correspondence and were very committed to resolving the problem at hand. I just couldn't stop thanking both of them for the relentless effort they were all putting in to get this sorted in time.

Each time I had the opportunity to speak with anyone of them, I would say thank you. Notably, the lady at the printing agency kept on saying to me, "You do not have to thank me, I have not done anything ... and, besides, I am simply doing my job."

Yet, I wouldn't stop thanking her and her colleagues for everything they had done so far. I told her, "Besides effectively communicating with us at each stage of the project, you have been liaising with our designer to ensure everything is ok and gets to you on time—something you are not obliged to do as it wasn't a part of your service to us … and for this, I am truly grateful."

On another occasion, when I expressed gratitude towards her and her team, she said, "We haven't done anything..."

I said, "Yes, you have done a lot, and whatever the outcome is – even if we do not manage to get the reviewed brochure to you on time to be printed for the launch – I am still very grateful for your service and support towards us." I kept assuring her that she had done so much to get us to this stage and that, regardless of what happened, we would be forever grateful for this act of kindness and empathy she and her team had shown towards us, irrespective of whether we got the leaflets in time for the launch or not.

After an hour or so, she sent me an email informing me that she would be going home at 5:30 p.m. but she would ensure that someone was in the office to hand over the brochures to me when they were done. Not knowing what to do or say anymore, I just kept saying, "Thank you, thank you, thank you... I am profoundly grateful." She then sent me another email, after having just spoken to me on the phone, saying that she just wanted to inform me that she was off now and leaving the office but had arranged for her colleague (whose name and contact number she also included in the email) to hand over the brochures to me on my arrival. I thanked her again for the great work. Then she added that her colleague was going to call me when the brochures were ready.

As I got ready to leave the office that evening, I received a phone call from a local number, which I immediately presumed was coming from their office. To my amazement, it was my local television studio calling to enquire if they could come and cover the launch of our new venture, which was a new health and well-being clinic. The journalist told me that they found the vision and objectives very timely and inspiring and believed it was a project worth sharing with the people of Liverpool. I was speechless and astonished by how quickly and effortlessly all this happened. Usually, I would have had to make several calls accompanied by emails to a handful of media/TV outlets in an effort to get them interested in our projects and events. Here I was, without a single email or call made, and the local TV was looking for us to broadcast our launch! In fact, I immediately accepted without giving it a second thought—and, of course, expressed gratitude to them! I kept on singing songs of thanksgiving as I prepared to leave the office that evening.

It was about 6:00 p.m. when I finally left the office and made my way to my car. As I got into my car, I received another phone call from the printing agency. This time, I was told that everything was ready and they were waiting for me to come and collect the brochures. I trusted the company and everything was perfectly packaged and handed to me on my arrival. I was profoundly humbled and grateful for their kindness towards me and my team. In fact, the brochures were flawless and spot on. The launch was a huge success and indeed one of our best launches ever—with very little effort on our part.

Now, why am I telling you all these stories? The reason behind these stories is to encourage and challenge you to practice gratitude in every given situation and/or storm in life and at all times—by sharing with you some personal real-life examples where the amazing power of gratitude was experienced in its most authentic and transformational form. Gratitude is a very rewarding and fulfilling/healthy lifestyle and choice. Whenever you show gratitude to those around you, they simply want to do more and may sometimes even go out of their way to support and encourage you with a joyful heart.

Gratitude instantly changes the dynamics of things and your circumstances and produces a sensation of assurance, fulfilment, and tranquillity. Furthermore, it has the power to unlock numerous doors of endless opportunities and favour available to you! It is absolutely and inevitably the ultimate garment and perfume to wear each time you step out of bed and your home! Never put a limit on the number of times you say thank you in a day. Let your ability to say thank you be bountiful and overflowing all day long...

REFLECTION & ACTION POINTS

Read the following questions gradually, reflect on them, and honestly write down your responses to them as evident in your life. Again the questions have been personalised.

1. Despite all that is going on right now in my life/or I may be going through in life at the moment, what one thing can I find in my life to be thankful and grateful for right now? I will write down more than one if I find more.

....

....

....

....

....

....

....

....

....

....

2.   What positive thing/s can I find in my current life situation/challenge to be thankful for?

....

....

....

....

....

....

....

....

....

....

3.   What can I do to express and demonstrate gratitude more often and daily?

....

....

....

....

....

....

....

....

....

....

4. Who can I call, write to, or talk to today to express my
    heartfelt gratitude to?

....

....

....

....

....

....

....

....

....

....

5. What can I thank myself for today and each new day?

....

....

....

....

....

....

....

....
....
....

6.   What can I thank my family for today and each new day? Ask yourself this question every single day.

....
....
....
....
....
....
....
....
....
....

7.   What can I thank my children for today?

....
....
....
....
....
....

....

....

....

....

8.   What can I thank my spouse for today?

....

....

....

....

....

....

....

....

....

9.   What can I thank my neighbour for today?

....

....

....

....

....

....

....
....
....
....

10. What can I thank a friend for today?

....
....
....
....
....
....
....
....
....
....

11. What can I thank my employer/ business partner for today?

....
....
....
....
....

....
....
....
....
....

12.   What can I thank my staff/colleague for today?

....
....
....
....
....
....
....
....
....
....

I greatly recommend you start executing this strategy straightaway after reading this chapter (if you have not been doing so yet) by cultivating a daily habit of thanksgiving. Every single morning, when you rise, endeavour to give thanks for the grace to see another new day—find at least three things to be grateful for before your feet touch the earth!

The fact that you made it to see this day and all the endless opportunities and possibilities it holds should never be taken for granted—many have not been as privileged and blessed as you are to see this wonderful and glorious day!

When you step out and encounter new and/or existing challenges and are about to be caught up in the turmoil, remind yourself again of that which you woke up in the morning being grateful for and of additional reasons and blessings in your life to be thankful for!

"A grateful heart is a beginning of greatness. It is an expression of humility. It is a foundation for the development of such virtues as prayer, faith, courage, contentment, happiness, love, and well-being." James E. Faust

This is dedicated to you ... especially in trying times and seasons. Sing or read aloud again and again – ensuring you count your blessings as you go – until you feel the assurance and peace within...

A Hymn of Gratitude by Johnson Oatman Jr.

When upon life's billows you are tempest tossed,

When you are discouraged, thinking all is lost,

Count your many blessings name them one by one,

And it will surprise you what the Lord hath done.

Refrain:

Count your blessings, name them one by one;

Count your blessings, see what God hath done;

Count your blessings, name them one by one,

And it will surprise you what the Lord hath done.

Are you ever burdened with a load of care?

Does the cross seem heavy you are called to bear?

Count your many blessings, every doubt will fly,

And you will be singing as the days go by.

Refrain

When you look at others with their lands and gold,

Think that Christ has promised you His wealth untold.

Count your many blessings, money cannot buy

Your reward in heaven, nor your Lord on high.

Refrain

So, amid the conflict whether great or small,

Do not be disheartened, God is over all;

Count your many blessings, angels will attend,

Help and comfort give you to your journey's end.

Refrain

Now, have you done all of the above and even more, yet the problem is still unresolved and you need to move forward but feel rather reluctant and extremely frustrated? Not to worry—this leads us to the next powerful strategy needed to enable you to achieve victory over the situation, which is The Power of Asking and Humility.

"Ask and it will be given to you; seek and you will find; knock and the door will be opened to you." Mathew 7:7

"We learned about gratitude and humility - that so many people had a hand in our success, from the teachers who inspired us to the janitors who kept our school clean... and we were taught to value everyone's contribution and treat everyone with respect." Michelle Obama

"True humility is intelligent self-respect which keeps us from thinking too highly or too meanly of ourselves. It makes us modest by reminding us how far we have come short of what we can be."

Ralph W. Sockman

CHAPTER SIX

The Power of Asking

Ask. Seek. Knock.

"Ask for help. Not because you are weak. But because you want to remain strong."

Les Brown

I am convinced that at this stage, when you must have tried it all and still are unable to overcome, you will definitely be less stressful because in it all you have been responding to the stressors ... and the feedback from your brain will definitely be different. Notwithstanding, you should know that man was never born to be alone or to live in isolation.

We were born to live in a community, in a society. We were born to live with one another and to complement one another. So, please, ASK for assistance! Ask, Seek, and Knock (ASK)! "Ask and you shall receive. Seek and you will find. Knock and the door shall be opened unto you." Mathew 7:7

Do not be afraid or feel humiliated to ask from others, asking is not a sign of weakness—rather it's a sign of courage, strength, and wanting to learn and know more. Furthermore, asking is a great sign of humility and surrender. In other words, you take the load and burden off your shoulder and surrender it/give it up so you may be lighter. Once the heavy burden that has been holding you back and keeping you down is shared, given up, or uplifted, you automatically feel lighter, relieved, less stressed, and can rise up and move forward again with less difficulty and greater ease.

Ask those who have undergone and overcome similar life challenges or crises. Ask about their experiences/how they affected them, and for the strategies they implemented to overcome the crisis you are currently undergoing and looking to overcome. Such people represent your role models, they are there to hold your hands and walk with you through the path and journey of recovery and victory—a path that they've once been through and are very familiar with.

Find out from them how they overcame the challenges and also ask those who are yet to overcome and find out how they are controlling and managing the situation. Ask as many questions as you can imagine. Find out from them how they are coping and moving on without being so overwhelmed. This interrogatory process will greatly help you—as you do not need to go through the same challenging pathways and/or make similar mistakes they made before you will be able to learn and rise above. One of my pastors once said this: "Learning from your mistakes is the lowest form of knowledge."

You could always learn from the experiences and mistakes of others—their mistakes could serve as a lesson and guidance to you. Indeed, they failed so you might succeed— as they will be your guide; they fell so you might rise up—as they will be your rock/stepping stone; and they endured so that you might thrive—as they will be the platform and springboard from which you take off.

Do not be afraid to ask for assistance, guidance, and/or direction when you get stuck or have tried everything possible to resolve the problem/challenge with no success. When you ask, one of these two things happens: you either have a positive response or a negative one.

However, the interesting thing is this: you actually lose nothing, even if the response is negative; you are simply in the same place or position you were in before asking, and maybe even better because you have learned something—a new skill perhaps, such as how to handle and overcome rejection. On the other hand, if the response is positive, then you have got a lot to gain—you are now in possession of something that you would never have had if you had not taken the time and courage to step out and ask. You should always remember that asking is a great strength and demonstrates your ability and willingness to learn and grow.

In addition, by asking, seeking, and knocking, you are indicating that you are willing to be patient and learn and not ready to give up just yet. It also shows that you are willing to acknowledge that you do not know it all, you do not have all the answers or know the pathway/s to the solution.

Nevertheless, you are willing to learn from someone who may know or have the answers—or knows how to arrive at the final destination and resolve the problem.

Furthermore, when you ask for assistance, it demonstrates that you have an in-depth knowledge of yourself and are fully aware of your full potential and capabilities and you are a confident person. It is great evidence that you are aware of and acknowledge your strengths, weaknesses, and limitations. It also reveals courage and attests that you are very conscious of the fact that you've now come to the edge of your limit—having done everything else you could have possibly done and within your power and ability without arriving at the expected solution or destination. Consequently, you now make a deliberate and conscious decision/choice to leverage, maximise and exploit the strengths, resources, and potential of friends, role models, professionals, and those around you/your network. You choose to let their strengths complement you and your weaknesses—this is wisdom, not stupidity!

Hence, by asking, seeking, and/or knocking, you are indulging in submission and acknowledging that you do not have the answers for everything that is happening in your life right now ... and this further demonstrates confidence in yourself and your ability to discern and make good judgement. In so doing, you also consciously or unconsciously acknowledge the fact that not having or knowing the answers or pathways to the solution of the problem does not necessarily mean that you are less intelligent or inferior in any way when compared to the individual and/or professional who knows the answers or path to the solution. On the contrary, it may simply indicate that you are aware of the fact that there are other people or professionals out there who could assist you to find the answers or different options and pathways that could eventually lead to the solution—thus taking the burden off you.

I am very aware of the fact that the one big/common obstacle that often holds many people back from asking is fear ... fear of rejection, fear of dismissal, and fear of being considered a failure, looser and/or sounding silly or foolish. You should never be afraid to ask, thus giving in to fear and letting it hold you back. There is absolutely no such thing as a foolish question. Every question is an opportunity to learn, grow, and become more knowledgeable and wiser. You would be amazed that even the most "silly" question enables us to learn some amazing and profound life lessons. Furthermore, the most foolish questions according to other people's perceptions might just turn out to be lifesaving. It might just be the one question that will take you to your final destination of resolution, fulfilment, and success—so ASK!

Ask, ask, and ask without ceasing—until it is given unto you. Do not give up. Do not take no to mean rejection. Look at it as another step closer to the next available option or prospect that will lead you to the solution. Never take any rejection or refusal personally. Most probably the person saying no to you genuinely cannot help you or is unable to resolve the problem—so keep pressing on and forward, searching for your next prospect, potential mentor, coach, and/or role model/champion. You are one step closer to getting the ideal help and solution to your problem/s.

Now, the questions you might be asking are these: "But who do I turn to for a solution or help? What help can I get to enable me or assist me overcome my current challenges or crises? Where can I find those willing and ready to help and support me? What doors can I knock at for opportunities and possibilities?"

The subsequent paragraphs are intended to provide you with a simple guideline, to assist and enable you identify where and/ or who you could ask from; who could support you; what support you could get in such situations/circumstances; and, finally, what doors of endless opportunities and possibilities are available and accessible to you to knock on.

Of note, there is currently no challenge in life that you have encountered or are currently encountering that is new or peculiar to you alone. Many have already encountered and overcome such challenges on their way to success, while others are also currently experiencing or encountering a similar challenge in their lives at this present time as you, and others are yet to encounter it. Therefore, you are not and will not be the only one in the world to actually encounter or experience such a challenge or mountain—so it will only be wise of you to ask from those who have already walked this path and are already at the top of the mountain, or at the end of the dark tunnel—where there is light.

You could approach and ask a friend whose strengths you know could meet the task or challenge at hand. However, one of the best categories of people/experts to ask guidance and support from are role models and mentors. A role model has been through a similar life situation and succeeded in overcoming it. Hence, they represent authentic testimonials that victory is possible and near and such challenges can be overcome by humans—since they, too, are mere humans, full of limitations as well as strengths just like you. They represent genuine testimonials and examples that could be used to support and guide you towards the solution and victory.

Consequently, you could then look to them for guidance and leadership. If they were once able to overcome that which to you may seem to be stumbling blocks, challenging, or even life threatening, then there is good news and hope for you—that you, too, can overcome and thrive! Hence, you should not be discouraged, neither should you be disappointed, sad, or depressed—there is still hope for you. Hope of a successful ending, hope of a grand finale. Hope that you, too, can, someday soon, overcome and thrive... Role models are there to hold your hands and walk with you. They are there to guide you through a similar path to that which they have been through or have in-depth knowledge about, and to help you climb up the stiff and rocky mountain or go through the long and narrow dark tunnel of despair. Other times, they are at the top of the mountain or at the exit of the tunnel, lending their hands out to you and waiting for you to join them—hence showing you that it is very possible to get to the top of the mountain, or to the end of the dark and narrow tunnel where there is light, despite all odds. Sometimes, they might even come down to meet you at your place and point of need because they are very familiar with the path or pathways that lead to the top of the mountain or to the end of the tunnel. They have walked the path – at times, not once, not twice, not thrice, but on numerous occasions – and are very confident in walking the path again—only this time with you!

Consequently, they are there to hold your hands and walk with you throughout the entire journey and pathway that leads to the top of the rocky mountain or to the end and exit of the long, narrow, and dark tunnel. They are there to show you the way and to ensure that you do not waste so much time and/or resources or make similar mistakes they or others have made in the past and, as a result, enable you to get there faster than they did or on time. They are there to show you the best way/direction that will take you down the most effective pathway that leads to victory. They are there to inspire and motivate you to take action, keep going, stay on track, and encourage/support you to always have your eyes fixed on the finish line, which in this case is the top of the mountain or the end of the tunnel—where there is victory. There they stand, patiently watching and waiting to celebrate your victory and rejoice with you.

A second category of persons or professionals you may also want to ask and seek assistance/guidance from are mentors— these are more experienced individuals than you with incredible potential and ability to see the very best in you and inspire and motivate you to take action and fulfil your maximum potential. Unlike a friend, who accepts and loves you just as you are, a mentor is someone who sees the very best of you and believes in you and in your ability to become the very best version of you and thrive!

"A lot of people have gone further in life to accomplish that which they never thought or believed they could, simply because someone else thought they could, believed in them, and inspired and encouraged them to do so—this is the role of a mentor."

Dr Sylvia Forchap Likambi.

"A mentor empowers a person to see a possible future, and believe it can be obtained." Shawn Hitchcock

You should never underestimate the role and power of a role model and/or mentor in your journey and quest to conquer and overcome. In your endeavour to overcome, this may just be the right time to find yourself a role model/mentor—if you do not have one yet. It is not sufficient to rely solely on yourself and/or friends/family and relations, especially when the challenge still remains unresolved; you have been given a wealth of resources and network for times like this! Make effective use of them!

The key difference between a friend/loved one or relation and a mentor is this: your friends/loved ones and relations see, accept, and love you for who you are—just as you are. On the contrary, a mentor sees the greatness within you and the great one that you are yet to become and could become—and consequently inspires, challenges, and motivates you to become that person and great individual that you truly are and that he/she sees in you!

In the subsequent parts of this chapter, I have identified and outlined other credible and experienced professionals and experts who are out there to help and support you overcome and thrive—hence, you could look out for them and ask them for guidance as well. These are professionals and experts with enormous expertise and experience in the field/area where you may currently be undergoing or encountering challenge. They have developed the skills and wisdom needed to support you in arriving at the most appropriate solution. They have mastered the best pathways to enable you to see and get to your final destination. In addition, they have also mastered the fields and pathways that you must avoid in order to have absolute victory and success.

They are a great resource to be leveraged in your journey to overcoming the challenges and the storms of life. They have spent a considerable amount of time learning and working to master the routes and/or map, such that at the very beginning of your journey to success and resolution you do not need to waste any more time doing this and can simply navigate through the right pathway. All you need to actually do is invest the time and resources needed to accomplish this and delegate to them the problem you have been trying to resolve without success—giving them the opportunity to execute that which they are well trained and qualified to do and, hence, know best. In addition, because they are not emotionally or physically involved, they are capable of remaining detached and very objective too—even in the midst of the challenge or crisis—a trait and quality that might otherwise be difficult for you to portray in your darkest and most challenging moments. The above professionals may fall under the category of coaches (life coaches, business/executive coaches, relationship coaches, career coaches, and communication experts), trainers, teachers, and counselors.

On the other hand, if you are a student or pupil, and the challenge you are currently facing is school related, then you might want to seek the assistance and support of your teacher/s or lecturer/s. They are definitely more knowledgeable than you in this area and therefore have the relevant and required skillset and knowledge, coupled with practical experience, to share with you and eventually support you and enable you to overcome whatever challenge/s you might be facing. It is their job to guide and assist you resolve some/or all of the problems you may encounter and/or experience while studying. Therefore, do not be afraid to ask for their assistance and consequently hold back and suffer in silence. Ask and you shall surely receive... You do not receive because you have not asked.

Now, when you have asked everyone you could possibly ask, searched everywhere you could possibly seek, and knocked on all the available and potential doors you could possibly knock on and, thus far, you still have not received or found the solutions or the answers to the problem, then here is your ultimate hope and source of ever-present help and support—Your Ultimate Source and The Mastermind Himself, The Greatest Mastermind behind your very creation, existence, and success, The Almighty God.

He sure knows and has all the answers. Just as a manufacturer knows his product and its potential extremely well, so, too, does your creator—God Almighty knows you extremely well. He knows exactly how He designed and equipped you to function on purpose so as to fulfil the role you were created and put here to accomplish. He knows just how to "fix you and your challenges" and restore you to your original state of being and well-being. He will re-establish you to your original mental, emotional, physical and spiritual state of well-being, harmony, and serenity so you may be able to experience and thrive in optimal health and wellness again!

Now, this takes us back in time, to the very beginning and first chapter of this book where we explored and discussed the power of "The Serenity Prayer". This is the ultimate moment for you to pray that magnificent and powerful prayer again... It is the time for you to completely surrender and simply ask, "Lord, grant me the serenity to accept the things I cannot change; the courage to change the things I can; and the wisdom to know the difference."

You must be conscious of the fact that it is of great relevance and significance for you to acquire "the wisdom to know the difference." In this way, you will be able to wisely establish whether or not this is a cause or battle you ought to fight and resist till the very end – and, hence, need the courage to do so – or whether it is simply one of those causes or battles that are not yours to fight—and consequently do not require you to invest your time, energy, and/or resources but rather require that you develop the resilience and serenity to accept and handle the situation with grace and peace. Therefore, wisdom is central and pivotal as it is the ability to know the difference. It represents your ability/capability to discern, pass judgement and make the right decision at the right time and place—always.

At this stage, whether the problem is resolved or still unresolved, by now, you should have established a sense of assurance and tranquility within you—knowing that everything is under control and everything works out for the good of those who love the Lord and are called according to His purpose. In effect, it may also be the case that you need the serenity within you to be able to let go of those changes that you cannot make or are not your duty and responsibility to make. Actually, it might just be the right time for you to let go of those things that are holding you back and look forward with great joy and determination to the life and amazing opportunities you have got ahead of you.

Ideally, now is the perfect timing for you to take a leap – with hope and faith – into a brighter and better future and not let your present challenges or storms hold you back or take control/shape and determine how your life goes and who you become. You must always bear this in mind: it is neither the challenges nor the experiences you encounter in life that shape and determine who you are or who you become in life. On the contrary, it is who you truly are and authentically represent that shapes and determines how you respond to those life challenges and storms that come your way.

Now, having surrendered everything to God (some say "The Universe," nonetheless, based on my faith and fundamental beliefs, I will make emphasis on God), there is the need to step back, review, analyse, and evaluate the situation/challenges such that you are able to draw life lessons out of them. Resolved or unresolved, you must be able to ask and find out what lessons you could take out of the situation and/or crises.

On the other hand, if you currently find yourself in a situation where doctors and medical professionals have told you that there is no longer anything that can be done about your situation or that pathological condition that you exhibit, I come to tell you this... Do not be troubled or despair. When there is no longer anything you or anyone else can do to bring about the ideal and desired solution, remember this... The one remaining thing to do and the one person left to turn to for timely help and intervention is The Divine Himself! Hand over every challenge/storm to Him and go about your activities without caring—being assured that "God is your refuge and your strength, an ever-present help in trouble." Psalms 46:1

Finally, I will end this chapter with this biblical story/parable that encourages us to pray always and be consistent in our asking—without ever giving up. In Luke 18:1-8, we are told of this amazing and very powerful story that encourages us to ask always and be very persistent, never giving up until a response is given unto us.

In this story we learn that: "In a certain town there was a judge who neither feared God nor cared about what people thought. And there was a widow in that town that kept coming to him with the plea, 'Grant me justice against my adversary.'

"For some time he refused. But finally he said to himself, 'Even though I don't fear God or care what people think, yet because this widow keeps bothering me, I will see that she gets justice, so that she won't eventually come and attack me!'

191

"And the Lord said, 'Listen to what the unjust judge says. And will not God bring about justice for his chosen ones, who cry out to him day and night? Will he keep putting them off? I tell you, he will see that they get justice, and quickly.'"

Food for thought: "However, when the Son of Man comes, will he find faith on the earth?"

REFLECTION & ACTION POINTS

1. What one thing do I need that I do not have in order to resolve my current challenge and/or crisis?

....
....
....
....
....
....
....
....
....
....

2. What one thing can I ask from someone today that will make a significant difference in my current situation?

....
....
....
....
....
....

....
....
....
....

3. Who is that one person, group, or organisation/institution that I could ask for assistance and guidance from concerning this problem/crisis today?

....
....
....
....
....
....
....
....
....
....

4. When and how can I ask and seek for such assistance and guidance?

....
....

....
....
....
....
....
....
....
....

5. What action/s or steps can I take to ensure that I step out
    and ask/seek for this support and guidance I have
    identified?

....
....
....
....
....
....
....
....
....
....

6. What knowledge can I seek today that will enable me to get closer to my ideal and desired solution/destination?

....

....

....

....

....

....

....

....

....

....

7. Where could I seek or acquire this knowledge from?

....

....

....

....

....

....

....

....

....

....

8. What new door/s of opportunities and possibilities can I
    knock on today?

....

....

....

....

....

....

....

....

....

....

9. Where can I find/locate these doors of opportunities and
    possibilities?

....

....

....

....

....

....

....

....

....

....

10. What more can I ask for today, tomorrow, next week,
     next month, etc.? What else?

Write them down as they come to your mind, initially in no
particular order. Then, subsequently, regroup them in order of
priority and significance by allocating numbers to them –
where the number 1 represents the most significant/important
thing you should ask for and that takes priority/precedence
over all the others – ensuring that you arrive at your final
destination on time and avoid any significant negative
consequence/s.

....

....

....

....

....

....

....

....

....

....

CHAPTER SEVEN

The Power of Wisdom

"How much better to get wisdom than gold, and good judgment than silver!"

Proverbs 16:16

"Never walk away from failure. On the contrary, study it carefully and imaginatively for its hidden assets." Michael Korda

"Some of the best lessons we ever learn we learn from our mistakes and failures. The error of the past is the wisdom of the future." Tryon Edwards

Now let's progress further and look at the next powerful strategy for overcoming life's challenges, which is

201

none other than The Power of Wisdom. As discussed at the very beginning of this book, challenges come to us to make us learn, grow, and become better and wiser. You are never meant to complete a challenging life journey or life experience and stay exactly the same way you were before embarking on that journey or encountering that challenge. All experiences lived are vital life lessons, both for us and for others to become wise.

Wisdom is the discernment between right and wrong, good and bad, truth and lie, etc., while knowledge is the acquisition of both. You must be conscious of the fact that not all knowledge acquired over time is vital and pivotal in transforming your circumstances and life. This is so because you might as well be getting knowledge that is not true but false. Of note, only knowledge of the truth could be vital and pivotal in bringing about true transformation and liberation from within us. "Then you will know the truth, and the truth will set you free." John 8:32 Knowledge is simply the acquisition of information – both true and false information – while wisdom is the application of knowledge of the truth or the right information acquired.

"Knowledge without application is irrelevant and without power...Knowledge without wisdom is irrelevant and of no use!" Dr Sylvia Forchap-Likambi

"Of note, Knowledge comes, but wisdom lingers." Alfred Lord Tennyson

"Some of the best lessons we ever learn we learn from our mistakes and failures. The error of the past is the wisdom of the future." Tryon Edwards

"...Wisdom is the principal thing; therefore get wisdom: and with all thy getting get understanding" Proverbs 4:7

Because wisdom is a practical thing, and comes from deep self-reflection, spiritual growth and revelation, I will write no further on this. My key objective is to arouse your appetite and thirst for wisdom, such that you hunger and desire it so badly and above all else. In this way, you become zealous and unstoppable in your search for wisdom … and, once found, you hold on to it—making it your best and most reliable companion and ally at all times.

Hence, now is the time to ask yourself these very profound questions and reflect on them. Take some time to reflect and ask yourself the following questions while letting your inner intuition and wisdom of The Holy Spirit within you guard you and your responses to the questions:

"What lessons can I draw out of this challenging life situation/experience that will help me now and in the future—in case I am confronted by a similar challenge again in life?"

"What message can I draw from this and, hence, communicate to others to help them overcome or avoid a similar challenge or crisis in their life?"

It is very fundamental to look for lessons in the midst of adversity/life storms and, above all, learn from them so you may be able to confidently move on to the next level. If nothing is learnt from the experience then you simply do not grow and stay at the same level and as the same old person that you were prior to encountering the challenge. As a result, when a similar life challenge or crisis comes your way again, you will struggle to overcome it and will have to start the process all over again—what a waste of valuable time, effort, and resources.

What benefit is it to you to get knowledge and not apply it or put it into practice? What good is it to you to spend a significant amount of your time and effort reading through this book yet never apply a single strategy in your life? It will be of absolutely no use and value to you!

Without identifying and learning the lessons entangled or wrapped up in each life challenge/crisis you face daily or occasionally there is no growth and you are therefore bound to stay as you are, shrinking with time as the challenge grows bigger, and, as a result, you will certainly be faced with similar life challenges over and over again—until you are ready to learn from them and move on or they eventually take hold and total control of you and your life.

However, when you look for lessons in the storm, and eventually learn from them, such lessons learnt are stored in your memory cells/subconscious mind. Consequently, when faced with a similar life challenge in the future, you are immediately prompted and reminded of what happened in the past and how it was encountered and overcome. You are also reminded of what skills, strengths, and strategies were employed and what mistakes were made in coping with and/or overcoming and triumphing over the situation. In this way, you are less fearful, not anxious, and more confident and serene in confronting and dealing with the present challenge—tapping into your already present potentials, strengths, knowledge, and experience.

For example, let's go back and take a look at the case of the daughter who was considered naughty and disrespectful—maybe the simple lesson or message to draw from this experience is this: she feels neglected and isolated by her mum/parents and they need to start spending more quality time with her. Hence, if you are currently experiencing a similar challenge with your daughter/child, it could be possible that, just like that mum, the core reason why you are currently going through this challenge/experience at the moment is so that you can eventually come to an awareness and understanding that you need to dedicate and spend more time with your daughter! Or maybe it is simply meant to educate or remind you of the significance of expressing your love for her daily.

Whereas in the case of that critical friend or spouse, the lesson to draw from this may be as simple as: you need to start trusting yourself and your ability to make the right choices and judgement more than you trust others and their perceptions and judgement about you. An additional lesson could be that you need the wisdom/spirit of discernment to guide and lead you when choosing your friends and life companion/spouse. Just as not everyone in the world can be your friend, in the same manner not every gentleman or beautiful lady who shows up to you is qualified to become your life companion/spouse. You need to always take time out and reflect, pray, seek your inner intuition and the wisdom of God before making such important life decisions—which should always align with your core beliefs and values.

On the other hand, the lesson may just be that you need to learn to forgive and let go more often in life. Whatever that lesson may be, your role is to identify, acknowledge and embrace it with an open mind and heart— with the willingness to start applying it in your life immediately and without delay in whatever sphere or area of your life it could be most relevant and beneficial.

Now, if all that is said and explored in this book has been done and applied consistently and ceremoniously yet you seem to be nowhere close to the solution or your final destination, and life seems to be taking a toll on you and it seems like you are almost giving up, and thinking, *Maybe these strategies are simply not for me as they are absolutely not working for me,* then one thing I am very sure of, and will tell you right now with unwavering confidence, is this: even though you might not have resolved the problem yet or arrived at your ideal solution/final destination yet, nonetheless, rest assured that you will experience more inner peace, insight, and find the mental strength and the courage to move on with serenity in other areas of your life—and, more often than not, even in the area of your life where you were or are currently experiencing challenge/s. By now, you must have become more resilient and tenacious.

Therefore, I urge and encourage you not to give up just yet—to try these well tested and proven strategies provided in this book day in day out each time you are faced with a challenging problem or crisis in life, and step back and watch your life and mindset be transformed for the better. At this stage, you may want to try implementing the strategies all over again from the beginning—but the key difference is you are a different person now and at a different position from that which you were, with a different mindset from that which you had at the very beginning when you first encountered the challenge/crisis and had not yet read this powerful manual/resource book. As a result of all these experiences, you are more knowledgeable, alert, and wiser and can therefore see clearer than you did before.

In this way, you are now capable of looking away from the challenge and focusing on you—looking and searching deep within, which then leads you once more to the very beginning of our powerful life changing strategies—the power of reflection (the first powerful strategy outlined and examined in this book). At this stage, you are once more called to be still, reflect, and pray the Serenity Prayer. "Lord, grant me the serenity to accept the things I cannot change, the courage to change things I can and the wisdom to know the difference."

Remember that peace is not the absence of war or crises but your ability to remain peaceful and serene in the midst of such. You can find and have peace even in the midst of your storms and darkest moments. The ultimate peace is that which dwells within you and surpasses all human understanding; that which produces hope and power—even in the midst of storms and life challenges.

"Inner peace begins the moment you choose not to allow another person or event to control your emotions." Pema Chodron

"The greatest misfortune that can come to a human being is to lose his inner peace. No outer force can rob him of it. It is his own thoughts, his own actions that rob him of it." Sir Chinmoy

Therefore regardless of whether or not you have arrived at the desired solution at this point in time, you must make the conscious effort and decision to be in control of the situation and circumstances surrounding you and not let the situation or circumstances/events control you/your emotions and overall well-being. Remember, happiness is a deliberate choice and lifestyle—not an event. Hence, you must be in the position now to choose happiness over sadness and peace over unrest, strife, or war.

I am here to remind you that it is neither the things that others say about you, your past or present hardships, struggles, challenges nor the things that happen to you in life that shape and determine who you are and your destiny. Rather, it how you respond to these hardships, challenges, critics, and the things that happen to you in life that determines who you are and your destiny.

In other words, you cannot keep making excuses or justifying your past or present circumstances and hold them responsible for who you are today or will become tomorrow/in the future. Thousands have gone through similar situations and hardships and have completely exploited and transformed them for their benefit ... and if they could do this, then you can too.

I have a very special message for you... Today, I urge you to simply let the mountains in your life become stepping stones or steps that will lead you to greatness rather than obstacles, stumbling blocks, and barriers that prevent you from attaining greatness. You are a victor and not a victim ... a winner and not a loser ... a success and not a failure ... a testimonial and not a statistic ... a very wise and intelligent being and magnificent creation of The Almighty God.

"In times of change learners inherit the earth; while the learned find themselves beautifully equipped to deal with a world that no longer exists." Eric Hoffer

"Never become so much of an expert that you stop gaining expertise. View life as a continuous learning experience."
Denis Waitley

REFLECTION & ACTION POINTS

1. Can I find any lessons to learn from this situation, challenge, and/or crisis? If yes, what one thing or lesson have I learnt from this?

....

....

....

....

....

....

....

....

....

....

....

....

....

....

....

....

....

....

2.   What lessons can I draw from this situation?

Now write down all the lessons you may have learned from this challenging situation, regardless of how insignificant those lessons may appear to you. No knowledge is ever wasted.

....

....

....

....

....

....

....

....

....

....

3.   How do these lessons apply to my life or how could they be relevant in my life?

....

....

....

....

....
....
....
....
....
....

4.   What use could I make of these lessons? How could I
      explore and exploit the wisdom entrapped within the
      lessons and apply that wisdom in my life?

....
....
....
....
....
....
....
....
....
....
....
....
....

5. How can I maximise the experience and lessons learned to enable me to become wiser, more resilient, and serene?

....
....
....
....
....
....
....
....
....
....

6. How could these lessons be exploited as a guide to help me avoid/encounter similar circumstances or challenges in the future?

....
....
....
....
....
....

....

....

....

....

7. How could I use them to effectively serve and impact
    others who find themselves in similar life situations?

....

....

....

....

....

....

....

....

....

....

At this stage, I am hoping that the problem has been
completely resolved; if not, I am hoping you are more calm,
less anxious/worried, and looking within and around you to
gather insights and lessons from your experience/s that will
enable you move forward without letting the setback hold you
back but, rather, exploiting it as the perfect opportunity and

platform for a comeback, bounce back, and spring forward. For this to be possible and sustainable, I have included a bonus and very handy strategy and lifestyle for you to incorporate henceforth. This final strategy will enable you develop and establish a resilient and serene mindset—a mindset that is able to accept the things that you cannot change and fuels you with the necessary energy and courage to change those things that you can change – without giving up – through positive affirmations.

"The greatest misfortune that can come to a human being is to lose his inner peace. No outer force can rob him of it. It is his own thoughts, his own actions that rob him of it." Sir Chinmoy

BONUS CHAPTER

The Power of Positive Affirmation

"Our thoughts and imagination are the only real limits to our possibilities."

Orison Swett Marden

Have you done everything previously outlined and discussed in this book and still have not arrived at the solution of the problem or acquired the serenity and mental strength required to achieve your goals and create an environment or platform for growth and personal development? Do not beat yourself up and get all frustrated and desperate—you must come to an understanding that you can overcome all things as long as you believe and have faith ... and this too shall pass. "If you can believe, all things are possible to him who believes." Mark 9:23. Nonetheless, if you are one of those who find it hard to believe this, or are unable to believe for whatever reason/s, all you need to do is simply suspend your disbelief/skepticism, like the father of the child in Mark 9:24 who cried out and said with tears, "Lord, I believe; help my unbelief!"

This last bit and final chapter is designed and written to equip you with powerful tools and resources that will encourage you to remain steadfast, optimistic, and confident at all times, no matter what. Your last bet is to have faith that everything happens for a reason and that every challenge that comes your way is for your good. "And we know that God causes everything to work together for the good of those who love God and are called according to his purpose for them." Romans 8:28 (New Living Translation). Hence, you should never give up faith in yourself and in your ability to overcome and thrive while in the midst of the challenge ... and most especially put your faith in God, and He will never leave, abandon, or forsake you. Also, remember that you are never a victim but always a victor—though this might not be evident initially.

In this final section, you are greatly encouraged to explore, exploit, and maximise the power of positive affirmations; incorporate them into your daily routine/life and apply them every morning and as often as required—even while still in the midst of the challenging situation or storm.

Affirmation is simply the action or process of affirming/guaranteeing something. You must remember that "The tongue has the power of life and death, and those who love it will eat its fruit." Proverbs 18:21.

Consequently, by affirming, you are merely speaking and bringing life into every dead situation and condition in your life. You are bringing hope where there was hopelessness; love where there was hatred; forgiveness where there was unforgiveness; healing where there was infirmity; peace where there was strife; order where there was confusion; and joy where there was sadness... Through the power of positive affirmations, you are using your words powerfully to create your new and ideal reality and experience.

Of note, science supports and endorses the power of positive affirmations. When consciously, deliberately, and repeatedly practiced, they have the potential to reinforce chemical pathways in the brain and strengthen neural connections. Furthermore, neuroscience has demonstrated that our thoughts are capable of changing the structure/neuroplasticity and function of our brains.

David J. Hellerstein, a professor of clinical psychiatry at The Columbia University, had this to say, "In brief, we have realized that 'neuroplasticity,' the ongoing remodeling of brain structure and function, occurs throughout life. It can be affected by life experiences, genes, biological agents, and by behaviour, as well as by thought patterns." Consequently, by practicing positive thought patterns (also known as affirmations) you actually create neuroplasticity in the area of the brain that processes what you are thinking about. For this to be effective, repetition of such thoughts is very crucial—as the process of repetition not only causes an overflow of positive thoughts within your brain but also results in the establishment of a habit and lifestyle, which eventually shapes and defines your actions and destiny. Furthermore, by constantly repeating such affirmations, whether or not you initially believe in them, you create an opportunity for such words and thoughts to be filtered through your conscious mind and stored in your subconscious mind.

"The abilities of this innate intelligence, subconscious mind, or spiritual nature are far greater than any pill, therapy, or treatment, and it is only waiting for our permission to willfully act. We are riding on the back of a giant, and we're getting a free ride."

Joe Dispenza

Once in your subconscious mind, they become your fundamental core beliefs that eventually shape and determine your values, words, actions, and habits. In effect, there is positive feedback and an amplification of your words/affirmations, which eventually give birth to your reality and destiny. At this advanced stage, regardless of how dark and hopeless your condition may be, you unconsciously and effortlessly speak light, hope, and life into it, out of the abundance and overflow of your heart and mind!

In order for this to be highly effective, I would recommend you choose one or two affirmations each day to focus on throughout the entire day. You should declare these affirmations several times within the day, and most importantly before going to bed at night. Of note, it is crucial that you speak aloud and in a very confident voice. The loudest voice in your mind will always prevail. In addition, by hearing yourself speak these words over and over, you build and develop your faith ... for faith comes by hearing...

"Now faith is confidence in what we hope for and assurance about what we do not see." (Hebrews 11:1).

To give more power to your affirmation and make it become a tangible reality that you can see, touch, and feel you must write it down and visualise it as you speak. Furthermore, while writing down your affirmations, you must ensure they are written in the present tense and are personal, as though they are your current reality, and refer to those things that are not fact as though they were.

In the subsequent parts of this chapter, I have put together a variety of positive affirmations for you to readily access and use every single day and as often as you can.

Endeavour to train yourself to use them every morning when you wake up/before stepping out of the house and at regular intervals during the day—until you develop the habit of doing so effortlessly and frequently. Every single day, you should repeat these positive affirmations to yourself, whether you initially believe them or not—until you get to the stage where you eventually start believing them. Remember, faith comes by hearing and the more you speak to yourself and repeat these positive affirmations, the more you hear them and start having faith and believing in them—irrespective of your current circumstances or what goes on within and around you.

Use the powerful and positive affirmations outlined below to instantly transform your thought patterns and reality. You are very welcome to apply them in any order of preference or certainty. Now write down each one of your chosen affirmations from the list on a sheet of paper and place it where there is great visibility—reading them aloud as often as you can...

1.   I am a victor and not a victim.

2. I am more than a conqueror through Christ who strengthens me.

3. I love myself more and more with each new day.

4. I am powerful and strong.

5. With each new day, I become the best version of myself.

6. I am very proud of who I am, where I have come from, and where I am now.

7. I acknowledge myself and all the progress I make.

8. I am beautiful just as I am.

9. Life is a beautiful gift, which I love, cherish, and appreciate.

10. I choose to make the very best of this current situation.

11. I choose to embrace each new day and moment of life with grace and love.

12. I forgive myself now and always.

13. I forgive others now and always.

14. I choose to appreciate The Now.

15. I choose to let go of yesterday and live in the present.

16. I am that I am, a very unique and divine creation destined for wonders and greatness.

17. I am the change I want to see and experience in my life and in the world.

18. I embrace every new challenge as an opportunity to grow and soar to greater heights.

19. I keep soaring to greater heights with each obstacle and barrier working in my favour.

20. I am becoming the very best version of myself with each new day.

21. I am more than a conqueror.

22. I am an embodiment of peace.

23. I am an embodiment of light.

24. I am an embodiment of love, joy, and patience.

25. My words are life; I will use my words to build my life and the life of others.

26. I am the happiest and most blessed individual on Earth.

27. I am an embodiment of kindness and gentleness.

28. Even in the midst of my greatest weaknesses, I am a conqueror.

29. I have incredible mental, emotional, and physical strength.

30. My strengths are my most valuable possessions required to excel and thrive in life.

31. I know and believe that whatever I ask and have faith in I shall receive.

32. I am a blessing and channel for positive change.

33. I acknowledge that faith is the substance of things hoped for and evidence of things not seen. Therefore I reignite my hope daily.

34. I am confident that my best days are still ahead of me and yet to come.

35. Happiness is my birthright. I receive happiness today and always as my present state of being.

36. I am happy now and always and have total control of my emotions and state of being.

37. I wake up this morning with a grateful and cheerful heart, full of love and passion for life.

38. I am a source of joy, love, and peace.

39. I have the power and ability to tap into my spirit and connect with the Holy Spirit in me, enjoying an abundance of joy, love, and peace—wherever and whenever I desire.

40. I represent a ray of light and hope for others.

41. I am happiness and joy in its purest form and inspire everyone around me to be happy.

42. When I look at my life and the world around me, my heart is filled with joy and gratitude.

43. I find joy and happiness in the most basic things of life and nature.

44. I love and enjoy life every single day.

45. I love laughing and having fun always, no matter what, and I represent an authentic source of humour, love, and happiness.

46. My heart overflows with love towards myself and towards others.

47. I have complete peace and assurance within me.

48. I expect to be successful in all of my endeavours.

49. Success is my birthright and I am always successful.

50. I am very solution-focused and capable of overcoming every life challenge I face.

51. I approve of and embrace myself now and always— just as I am.

52. I am perfectly imperfect and love my imperfect human nature.

53. I love myself profoundly and unconditionally.

54. I forgive myself completely and wholly now and always.

55. I am unique and special. I am blessed and grateful to be alive and to be me.

56. I trust and profoundly believe in myself and I am very confident in my inner wisdom and ability to make the right judgement.

57. I am a person of great integrity; I am always loyal and totally reliable. I am confident I must overcome this situation.

58. I take full responsibility for my life and the transformational power within me.

59. I act from a place of personal conviction and assurance.

60. I am grounded in my life, as is my spirit.

61. It is very safe for me to be still and at rest.

62. No human knows me better than I know myself; hence, I know what is best for me.

63. I alone know my thoughts and have constant access to them. I therefore choose to always think positively, no matter what.

64. I fully accept myself and know that I am worthy of greatness.

65. As I love and approve of myself and others, my life and experiences get better and better.

66. I release all that is unlike the action of love and receive love and joy in abundance.

67. I am willing and ready to change the pattern/s in me that created this condition.

68. I love my life.

69. I choose to be proud of myself. I am expressing and receiving joy.

70. I am experiencing deep inner peace within me.

71. I choose to constantly feed my mind with positive and nourishing thoughts.

72. I live in the moment and appreciate everything and every being that is a part of now with love, compassion, and kindness.

73. My mistakes and setbacks are stepping stones to my success because I learn from them daily.

74. Every day is a new beginning and a new opportunity for me to thrive and become the best version of myself.

75. I know exactly what I need to do to achieve success and victory. I am in control.

76. I am always valuable and worthy.

77. I am salt to the earth and will retain my saltiness at all times.

78. I am light to the world and will never dim my light, no matter what. I continually shine to benefit myself and others.

79. I am strong, I am courageous, and I am powerful—at all times.

80. With every fall and setback I come back greater—rising even higher and becoming more resilient.

81. I am pure dynamic energy.

82. My purpose is to succeed in all that I do and know that success is a reality awaiting my arrival.

83. I have a spirit of love, sound mind and courage and not a spirit of fear! I am fearless and courageous.

84. I feel powerful, capable, confident, energetic, and at my very best. I am amazingly happy.

85. I love challenges that stretch me and approach them with boldness and enthusiasm.

86. I live in the present and I am confident of a bright and prosperous future.

87. I am a very confident individual; I am bold, friendly, and outgoing.

88. I am independent, creative, persistent, and consistent in all that I do.

89. I am energetic, bubbly, passionate, and enthusiastic at all times.

90. I always attract only the best of circumstances and the most positive and optimistic people in my life.

91. I consciously choose to see only the very best in myself and in others, regardless of what is going on around me.

92. I am a problem solver. I focus on solutions and always find the best solution and way out of any problem.

93. I love change, I am a change agent, and very easily adjust myself to new situations and environments.

94. My body, soul, and spirit are in complete harmony, which results in an overall sense of peace and serenity in my being.

95. I flourish in optimal mental, emotional, physical, and spiritual health and well-being.

96. I am convinced that my thoughts become my reality, and therefore I can create my new and ideal reality by changing my thoughts to match the reality I desire.

97. With each new challenge, I become more and more confident, wiser, and better.

98. I am physically and physiologically strong and healthy, equipped and prepared to overcome every threat and challenge.

99. Every morning, I nourish my body with healthy food and drink, my mind with healthy and positive thoughts and words, and my spirit with unconditional love and everlasting peace.

100. I have the power and authority conferred to me by The Divine to overcome every pain in my body and heal myself from within.

101. I now live beyond other people's fears and limitations, including mine.

102. I am peaceful, loving, kind, and happy, and everyone loves and enjoys my company.

103. I am sowing seeds of love, peace, kindness, joy, self-control, patience and compassion wherever I am—and must surely reap these in harvest season.

104. My home and surrounding environment are calm and peaceful.

105. I release anger, pain, and hurt and fill myself with an abundance of love, serenity, and peaceful thoughts.

106. All is well with my soul right now.

107. I am very grateful for this moment and find joy and meaning in it.

108. I gently and easily return to a state of complete harmony and peace.

109. I am very aware of my own thoughts, actions, and limitations; I accept and embrace them without passing judgement.

110. I live fully in the present, I appreciate every moment and choose to let go of the hurt and disappointment of the past.

111. Life is in the moment; I live and cherish every moment as if it were my last and most precious.

112. I accept, embrace, and live all experiences, even unpleasant ones, taking with me the lessons and wisdom drawn from them.

113. I am objective; I can perceive and control my emotions without getting attached to them.

114. I meditate daily and without resistance or anxiety on the promises of the Word of God, which is food for my soul.

115. I am serene and at peace with everyone and everything in my life. With every breath I take I feel a deep sense of inner peace that surpasses all human understanding.

116. Every day I get better and better and stronger and stronger.

117. I know that everything works out for my good and according to God's purpose and plan for my life.

118. Being in a state of harmony and calmness energizes my whole being.

119. Even when there is chaos and unrest around me, I remain calm and focused on me and the peace within me.

120. I overcome and defeat stress and anxiety of any kind. I live in peace.

121. I am free of anxiety and a calm inner peace fills my entire being and soul.

122. All is well in my life. I am serene, happy, and contented—just as I am.

123. My body is healthy; my mind is brilliant; my soul is tranquil.

124. I am superior to every negative thought and mediocre action.

125. I forgive all those who have hurt and oppressed me in my past and peacefully detach from them and the experience.

126. An overflow of love and tranquility is washing away my anger and replacing it with love, kindness, and gentleness.

127. I am guided in my every step by The Holy Spirit that dwells in me and leads me towards what I must know and do.

128. Happiness is a deliberate choice. I choose to be happy as a result of my own accomplishments and the blessings I've been given.

129. My ability to conquer my challenges is limitless; my potential to succeed is infinite.

130. I am courageous and I can stand up for myself and for others who are weak and fearful.

131. I am living a glorious and fulfilled life—my best life ever.

132. I love my life and all of my experiences, good and bad, and I will never trade my life for anyone else's, no matter what.

133. Many people look up to me for counsel, guidance, and direction and recognise my worth; I am valued, respected, and admired.

134. I am blessed with an incredible life, family, and amazing friends.

135. Everything that is happening now is happening for my ultimate good.

136. Though these times are very challenging and difficult, I fully recognise that they are merely seasons and events and shall surely pass.

137. I am conquering every challenge I encounter; I am overcoming it steadily and with grace.

138. Every barrier and wall in front of me is gradually transforming into a bridge/gateway that connects me to my destiny. I therefore walk in faith.

139. Every obstacle around me and my surroundings are gradually turning around and moving out of my vicinity; my path is designed towards greatness and victory.

140. I am perfectly at peace with everything that has happened in my past, is happening right now, and will happen in the future—shalom.

141. I am an eagle with a great vision that takes me beyond my physical limitations and empowers me with an incredible ability to soar to greater heights in the midst of storms.

142. I am a spiritual being created in the magnificent image of God Almighty.

Make maximum use of the above affirmations as often as you can—the more often you employ them, the more productive and life changing they become. You are encouraged to use them even when you do not have any problem or challenge to overcome. They are vital for the nourishment of your mind/soul, spirit, and body and for the building of your faith and resilience. Remember, faith comes by hearing...

Take note that the above affirmations are not for you to examine, analyse, and evaluate whether or not they are true and apply in your life or circumstances. Also, it is not a prerequisite that you completely believe in every one of them. They are simply for your usage—whether they apply in your life or not. All I ask is that you have an open and non-critical mind, suspending every un-belief for now—and just use them daily!

You can utilize any of the affirmations you choose to, either alone or in combination with one or more of the others, in order to suit your personal needs and demands. However, it is important and vital to establish a profound communication system through which the affirmations will be communicated and allowed to express themselves in reality. Hence, confess and say them with conviction so they may eventually become a reality.

Always remember this: words are powerful and the power of life and death lies in the tongue. Therefore, this is your unique opportunity and chance to use your words to bring life to every dead situation and event. Use your words to create those things that are not so they can become a tangible reality. It is your ultimate chance to shape and determine your destiny and create the life and future that you desire and deserve—amidst all odds.

"Tell me and I forget, teach me and I may remember, involve me and I learn." Benjamin Franklin

This is your chance and opportunity to be proactively involved in the ultimate resolution and healing process of your life. No one can make change happen for you. Irrespective of how much I love you and desire to impact and transform your life, I can't do this for you. The choice is yours and yours only. You must bring about the change you envisage and hope for. You are either an agent of change or a victim of change and with or without your input change will happen anyway. Therefore, you are better off becoming an agent of change and playing an integral part in the change agenda and plan for your life. This is a lifelong and never-ending journey—a journey of change, a journey of hope, a journey of transformation and of continuous growth and personal development... Therefore be proactive at all times and avoid being reactive!

Consider all of the above affirmations as seeds of greatness and victory that you are sowing in your life. Therefore, all you are required to do is to take the seeds and sow now! What happens after that should neither be your concern nor preoccupy you. One thing is certain, whatever you sow you will reap and in abundance too! Therefore, if you have sown, be certain to reap the fruits in abundance in the season of harvest. Such fruits will eventually benefit you and those around you.

Now that you have been given the seven fundamental keys and principles required to demolish every road block/blockage and unlock every closed door that leads to your destiny, I beseech you to accept with an open mind these life-changing keys that have the ultimate power and potential to change/transform your life and grant you access to victory and success/eternal peace. Henceforth, you must step out and apply them in the relevant areas of your life.

As you read these final and closing words of this book I strongly recommend that you do not immediately put the book away and go about your daily activities as normal... Let this be a transition moment in your life. Go forth with a renewed mindset and perception of life and let this be your manual, guide, and reference; let it encourage and direct you in how to go about living a glorious, happy, fulfilled, peaceful, and purposeful life—amidst all odds.

You Are Highly Blessed, Divinely Favored, And Destined For Greatness!

You are a victor and not a victim!